THE ART OF THE TOY SOLDIER

The Art of the Toy Soldier

Two Centuries of Metal Toy Soldiers 1770–1970

BY HENRY I. KURTZ and BURTT R. EHRLICH

Foreword by Roy Selwyn-Smith.
Text by Henry I. Kurtz.
Photography by Serge Nivelle.
Based primarily on the
Collection of Burtt R. Ehrlich.

New Cavendish Books

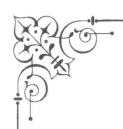

First edition published in Great Britain
by New Cavendish Books—1987

Photography—Serge Nivelle
Design—John B. Cooper
Editorial direction—Allen Levy

Production consultants—Abbeville Press.
Typesetting by Wyvern Typesetting Ltd, Bristol.
Printed and bound in Japan.

New Cavendish Books, 21–23 Craven Hill, London W2 3EN
Distribution: ABP, North Way, Andover, Hampshire.

ISBN 0 904568 44 X

Contents

Foreword

By ROY SELWYN-SMITH

"Toy soldier" is a term often frowned upon by the connoisseur collector of military miniatures; yet for volume production we must turn to past makers of little model figures that were originally toys for children and that now form the basis of one of the most intriguing and delightful hobbies: collecting old toy soldiers.

The charm of the old toy soldier lies in its simplicity of shape, which verges on that of a caricature. With his doll-like rosy cheeks and small black-dot eyes—unblinking, wide-awake—he seems to be awaiting your command in a fantasy world where his only claim to individuality is the slight variation of his bright, glossy uniform supplied by the painter's hand.

A new box of toy soldiers must have enthralled many a youngster, mesmerized by these tiny men in perfect order. Once he took them from their box, a young boy could review the little army from above, or, by lying at floor level, could march with them into battle. It is such childhood memories that are the start of many toy soldier collections.

For me the fascination of toy soldiers is not only the miniaturization of the military man but also the method by which he was made. When I examine a toy soldier, I look for the mold line and try to determine the shape of the mold from which he was cast. This stems from the many years I spent modeling originals for mass production by Britains Ltd. and other makers. The design problem is always the same: how to create a figure in an interesting position within the limitations imposed by a particular molding process.

Commercial manufacturers of toy soldiers were influenced by financial considerations and used many materials including tin, aluminum, plaster composition, papier-mâché, even a mixture of glue and pumice powder. However, the most common material was an alloy of lead and antimony. The weight of the metal had to be held to a minimum, relative to the strength of the figure, and the amount of paint and the variety of colors applied were kept within the limits of a carefully costed product. We now have the plastic toy soldier, but the same conflict of balancing price against quality continues.

Financial considerations also affect collectors, compelling even the most ardent among them to set boundaries. Some may concentrate on the figures of a preferred manufacturer, while others may collect only those of a particular period or army. My aim has been to keep at least some of the production models of my own creation; and these are an assorted collection of figures that I designed for Timpo, Zang, Herald, and Britains, as well as a few modeled for Richard Courtenay, Denny Stokes, and Otto Gottstein.

Past manufacturers of children's toys could not have foreseen the day when their little soldiers would be held in such high regard that a major book would be entirely devoted to them. Yet it is natural for the serious collector to seek out useful reference material that will aid him in the pursuit of his hobby; and although many books on model soldiers have been published, *The Art of the Toy Soldier* consolidates areas of existing research and also explores more fully the work of makers not previously covered in sufficient detail. For this reason, it is a most welcome addition to the bookshelves of both the established collector and the general reader with a fond regard for the toys of yesteryear.

Preface

More than thirty years ago, I received as a birthday gift a set of imported toy soldiers, made in England by the firm of Britains Ltd. To be precise, it was a set of the Coldstream Guards, utterly captivating in their towering bearskin hats and bright scarlet tunics. That initial set of Britains, purchased at a New York department store for the grand sum of $1.69, proved to be only the first of many such acquisitions. By the time I reached my early teens, I had assembled a small army of nearly 1,000 toy troops. When not engaged in playroom combat, they were neatly quartered in their original boxes, which eventually occupied much of the shelf space in my one closet. Most of the boxes carried the Britains trademark, but there were others marked Crescent, Mignot, and Authenticast—names well known to any serious toy soldier collector.

Decades have swept by since I maneuvered my little warriors across carpeted floors in mock battles and parades, and the times, as they always do, have changed. No longer will you find imported lead soldiers selling for less than $2 a set in local department stores. Old toy soldiers like the ones I played with have become collector's items; they have appreciated at a rate of 100 percent or more a year, with prices skyrocketing since the mid-1970s, and today sets sell at auction, and at shops specializing in military miniatures, for $75 and up. Some rare items command astronomical sums.

Thus, the lead soldiers of earlier generations have joined the ranks of tin toys and other virtually extinct forms of playthings as valuable collectibles. With their value rapidly increasing, old toy soldiers are now sought after by genuine enthusiasts as well as a new breed of investor-collectors, prompting the *Wall Street Journal* to observe recently that "toy soldiers have joined stamps, jewelry and fine art as investments."

My own interest in toy soldiers waned during my college years only to be revived during the course of preparing an article on the hobby for a national magazine. As I interviewed collectors and began attending toy soldier auctions and model figure society exhibitions, I felt a rekindling of the old spark. The "closet collector" in me emerged and I returned to the active duty roster.

One of the collectors who helped to reactivate my interest was Burtt R. Ehrlich, president of a New York fixed-income securities firm, who over a period of ten years has assembled one of the finest collections of toy soldiers to be found anywhere—numbering more than 15,000 figures. What makes the Ehrlich collection truly distinctive, however, is not its size—in fact, there are others containing far greater numbers of figures—but its quality and depth. The Ehrlich collection is well thought out. It has been put together with care, the result of Burtt's own extensive research and the advice of experts such as Steve Balkin, proprietor of the Burlington Antique Toy Shop in New York. Figures are never collected randomly, but always with a view toward adding a new dimension to the collection or filling an existing gap. As a result, the Ehrlich collection is truly of museum quality.

Early in our association, Burtt mentioned his interest in putting out a book on old toy soldiers that would be both visually and textually satisfying to the connoisseur collector, and that would use his collection as a primary resource. It seemed to both of us that a need existed for a book on toy soldiers comparable to the pictorially splendid *Art of the Tin Toy* and *Golden Age of Toys*. To fill that gap, we conceived the idea of this survey of two centuries of metal toy soldiers. It is our hope that this book will prove satisfying and useful to toy soldier collectors and others interested in antique toys and collectibles.

It must be stated at the outset that this book is neither a catalogue nor an encyclopedia. To do full justice to the hundreds of commercial toy soldier manufacturers that have flourished at one time or another during the past two centuries would require many volumes and an author with an extremely long life expectancy. Sensibly, I believe, we decided to concentrate on the principal makers of the four major toy-soldier-producing nations: Germany, France, Great Britain, and the United States. We can only apologize in advance to those collectors who feel slighted because a favorite firm has received insufficient recognition or—worse yet—has been omitted altogether. On the other side of the ledger, the product lines of leading makers such as Britains, Heyde, Mignot, Barclay, and Manoil are treated to far more extensive coverage and analysis than in most previous books on the subject.

Then, too, we must offer a cautionary note concerning statements made in text and captions about the height of specific toy soldiers. Measuring toy soldiers is at best an inexact science, the usual procedure being to calculate the distance between the base and the top of the head—not including headgear. Complicating the problem is the fact that figures often do not measure up to the size specifications given in manufacturers' catalogues. As a case in point, the popular "Size 2" figures of the Georg Heyde Company were supposed to be 52 millimeters in height. But when actually measured, most Heydes of this scale (especially those produced after World War I) are found to average between 48 and 50 millimeters. Similarly, the so-called Standard Size Britains models are said to be 54 millimeters, based on a 1:32 scale in which a normal-size man of 5 feet 8 inches is reduced to $2\frac{1}{8}$ inches (which translates to $\frac{3}{8}$ inch to 1 foot). But anyone who has ever measured a varied group of Standard Size Britains knows that 54 millimeters is a good guideline but not an absolute. To simplify matters, we have used official catalogue designations, so that, for example, Standard Size Britains foot

and mounted figures are deemed to be 54 and 70 millimeters respectively.

The efforts of many people made this book possible and I am happy to acknowledge their respective contributions. First and foremost, I would like to thank Burtt Ehrlich for encouraging me to write this book, for underwriting the initial editorial costs, and for making his marvelous collection available for research and photographic purposes. Both Burtt and I are much indebted to Serge Nivelle, a talented photographer whose excellent pictures capture the spirit of the little metal warriors described in the following pages.

As the author of the text, I am particularly grateful to the late John G. Garratt, the dean of writers on the subject of toy and model soldiers, who reviewed the entire manuscript and offered valuable suggestions for improving the text; to Peter Johnson, the author of *Toy Armies* and the curator of the Forbes Museum of Military Miniatures, in Tangier, Morocco, who scoured the manuscript for technical and typographical errors; to Morry Miles, editor of the British Model Soldier Society's journal *The Bulletin*, who delved into that group's files and came up with a series of splendid articles on Heyde and Mignot by the late L. W. Richards; and to Roy Selwyn-Smith, former deputy chairman of Britains Ltd., who patiently responded to a host of queries and who also provided photographs and other useful material from the company's archives.

Special thanks must go to the following individuals for their valuable contributions: Steve Balkin, who provided information about lesser-known companies as well as samples of their figures; Professor George Keester, a veritable fund of information about toy soldiers, who reviewed and amended the chapters on French and American manufacturers; Larry Levine, who graciously permitted us to photograph American dime-store figures from his outstanding collection; Michael McAfee of the West Point Museum, who furnished important reference material about the history of several American toy soldier firms; Richard O'Brien, author of *Collecting Toys*, who assisted me in the preparation of the section dealing with American dime-store companies; and Jo and Steve Sommers, comanaging editors of the *Old Toy Soldier Newsletter*, for many acts of cooperation and assistance.

Others who allowed me to pick their brains, or to pick through their collections, are: Søren Brunoe (my good friend and Denmark's leading model soldier maker), Michael Curley, Ake Dahlback (founder and curator of Sweden's Tennfigur Museum), Lee Daniels, Holger Eriksson, Robert Frye, president of the New York branch of Phillips, the fine-art auctioneers (for providing photographs of rare items), Gus Hansen, Victor Medcalf, Joanne and Ron Ruddell, Stewart Saxe, Ernest Schwartz (a very good friend, who cheerfully transported platoons of Authenticast, S.A.E., and Timpo figures from his collection to the photographer's studio), Joe Wallis, and Bill Lango, editor and publisher of *Toy Soldier Review*.

I am also happy to acknowledge the assistance of S. Ralph Cohen of Scandinavian Airlines System (SAS) for making possible a trip to Denmark and Sweden during which I did research on Scandinavian manufacturers. Else Rothe of the Danish Information Office generously gave of her time in translating source material in Danish and Swedish. Similarly, Dr. Rudolph Schwartz, a friend and fellow collector, translated portions of German-language books containing significant information about Austrian toy soldier firms. Finally, a big thanks to Jitka Salaquarda and Maureen McDonough for typing the manuscript and the captions for hundreds of photographs.

And now turn the page and enter the wonderful world of the old toy soldier.

HENRY I. KURTZ
New York City, 1987

Introduction

Toy soldiers! What is it about them that has fascinated generations of children—particularly, but not exclusively, young boys? There is no questioning the fact that the appeal of the toy soldier is universal, transcending national boundaries and diverse cultural backgrounds. Nor can it be denied that toy soldiers—a generic term, for there were also miniature civilians—have been, and still are, treasured by the tens of thousands who played with them in childhood and who now, as adult collectors, continue to revere them as nostalgic mementos.

It has been said that toy soldiers are charming and colorful, and that is certainly true. The spectacle of gaily garbed Scottish Highlanders or brilliantly bedecked hussars parading en masse can dazzle the viewer. But other toys are charming and pretty to behold. What is it, then, that makes the toy soldier an object of special affection for so many? And why, now that traditional lead soldiers have joined tin toys, bisque dolls, and other handcrafted playthings of yesteryear as collectibles, would a collector be willing to pay $11,000, as one recently did at a New York auction, for a single rare set of a Boer War-period British Army Supply Column by Britains, the most popular and prolific of the commercial manufacturers?

Part of the answer is provided by Michael J. McAfee, a curator at the West Point Museum, which recently mounted an exhibit surveying the history of the toy soldier. "To me," writes McAfee, "the charm of the figures as toys is coupled with their value as historical survivors of a lost era. I feel as compelled to preserve equally a battered 'veteran' of my childhood war games as I do a collector's mint piece. Both are historical evidence and should be preserved."

McAfee's remarks represent the more sophisticated overview of the adult collector. From the perspective of a child, however, toy soldiers fulfilled a more fundamental emotional need—they enabled him to create his own fantasy world in miniature. With a handful of toy soldiers, a youngster could imagine himself an all-powerful ruler of a Lilliputian world, whether leading thumb-sized soldiers in battle or running a miniature farm, zoo, or circus. It matters little what form the play took, only that it stretched the child's imagination. That element of creative play is also found in the adult collector, for as Steve Sommers, coeditor of the *Old Toy Soldier Newsletter*, points out: "Some collectors may arrange their figures in parade formation. Others may play with them by creating scenes and photographing them. It's all a form of play because it takes us away from reality to a world of fantasy."

It might fairly be said that even as the child grasped a toy soldier in his hand, he became an emotional captive of that tiny metal man. So it is not surprising that the discovery of a box of toy soldiers under a Christmas tree, or its presentation as a birthday gift, was a source of special delight. Hans Christian Andersen captured that precious moment in the opening lines of his short story "The Steadfast Tin Soldier":

There were once five and twenty tin soldiers, all brothers, for they had been made out of the same old tin spoon. They shouldered their muskets and they held themselves upright, and their uniforms were red and blue, very gay indeed. The first thing they heard in this world, when the lid was taken off their box, were the words "Tin soldiers!" The words were spoken by a little boy who clapped his hands with

← American Continentals confront British Grenadiers as they might have at the Battle of Saratoga. Heyde produced many sets of American Revolutionary War troops.
Burtt Ehrlich Collection   Height: 52 mm

delight. The soldiers had been given to him because it was his birthday, and straightaway he put them out on the table.

More than a century has passed since Andersen penned those lines, but the sentiment is timeless. For those who have experienced it, that precious moment when a box is opened and a child comes face-to-face with a squad of glossy-painted toy soldiers remains frozen in time in that corner of the mind where joyful occasions are forever preserved. Ask a toy soldier collector about his first set of "little people" and he will regale you with details: the distinct aroma of the waxy paper covering the box; the colorful lids proclaiming "Regiments of All Nations" or "Fabrique Française" or "Feine Compositions-Figuren"; and most of all the feel of the shiny metal man clutched firmly in hand.

John Garratt, whose books on model soldiers are well known to all serious collectors, recalls being introduced to toy soldiers at the tender age of four. During a visit to relatives in Liverpool, an older cousin produced a "large box of assorted lead soldiers" and, writes Garratt, "a happy time was had in arranging them on a table." Much to the young Garratt's dismay, however, when it was time to leave, the soldiers were put back in their box and returned to a cupboard. Describing the incident many years later, Garratt reported: "The profound shock of disappointment is still with us, and we still blush when we recall the tears and sobs that ensued, and how miraculously they ceased when the box was thrust into our willing hands. . . . The journey home through gas-lit Liverpool streets is still a rosy dream even though we have forgotten whether the troops were Britain's or Heyde's or Mignot's."

For some children, playing with toy soldiers was a casual venting of destructive impulses, with the little lead men being bombarded by rocks, marbles, and missiles fired from pellet guns and toy cannons. For others, it meant refighting the battles of history or creating fantasy wars. For those like H. G. Wells and Robert Louis Stevenson, who carried their childhood affection for toy soldiers into adulthood, it meant formulating complex rules of war gaming. H. G. Wells, of course, is well known for his books *Floor Games* and *Little Wars*, while Stevenson spent many of his leisure hours devising his own intricate form of *kriegspiel*. In an article published in the December 1898 issue of *Scribner's Magazine*, Lloyd Osbourne, Stevenson's stepson, provides us with an account of the author's deep involvement with toy soldiers during his convalescence from an illness at Davos Platz, Switzerland, in the early 1880s. According to Osbourne:

> The abiding spirit of the child was seldom shown in more lively fashion than in those days of exile at Davos . . . the printing press, the toy theatre, the tin soldiers all engaged his fancy. Of these, however, the tin soldiers most took his fancy; and the war game was constantly improved and elaborated, until from a few hours a "war" took weeks to play. . . . The mimic battalions marched and countermarched, changed by measured evolutions from column formation into line, with cavalry screens in front and massed supports behind, in the most approved military fashion of today. . . .

Wells and Stevenson are but two of the many prominent individuals with a special fondness for little lead troops. Historically, the ranks of those who have played with and collected toy soldiers include such diverse personalities as Charlotte and Emily Brontë, Sir Winston Churchill, Andrew Wyeth, and Douglas Fairbanks, Jr. Anatole France admitted practicing the "fetishism of lead soldiers"; and G. K. Chesterton, himself a toy soldier enthusiast, remarked in his autobiography that among the many books he thought of writing was one about a successful businessman who had a dark secret and "who was eventually discovered by the detectives still playing with dolls or tin soldiers. . . ."

Despite their widespread popularity, commercially made toy soldiers are a fairly recent addition to the world of children's playthings. Although miniature replicas of fighting men made out of clay, wood, and bronze were discovered in ancient Egyptian, Greek, and Roman tombs, these were mainly religious objects—part of what archaeologists categorize as tomb furniture—that may have doubled as childrens toys.

Up until the latter part of the 18th century, toy soldiers were mainly the playthings of the rich. During the Middle Ages, the sons and daughters of noblemen used wooden models of knights to stage mock tournaments. Strings and pulleys enabled the children to send the knights crashing into each other so that their lances actually broke, as in a real joust. In later centuries, toy replicas of soldiers were used to educate the sons of kings in the art of warfare. Often these royal playthings were made of silver or gold. As a young prince in the 17th century, Louis XIII of France had a magnificent set of 300 toy soldiers handcrafted in silver. This handsome set was passed on to his son, the future Louis XIV, who subsequently augmented his miniature army with additional troops mounted in such a way that they could actually maneuver and fight battles. From a contemporary account we learn that the silver soldiers "marched to left and to right, doubled their ranks, lowered their weapons, struck fire, shot off, and retreated."

Most toy soldiers of the 17th and 18th centuries were made of some type of metal. But many other materials were used, wood, cork, and wax among them. There were even toy soldiers that could be eaten. Made of sugar and flour, they were hardened in molds until firm enough to be painted. Like their civilian counterpart, the gingerbread man, they were quite popular. As a boy, Czar Peter III had an entire collection of these pastry soldiers. One time, according to a popular story, he discovered that a rat had raided the royal cookie jar and had eaten part of his army. A furious Peter ordered his royal guardsmen to capture the rat, and then had it court-martialed and executed.

Until the 18th century, toy soldiers remained, for the most part, an item only the very rich could afford. Beginning in the early 1700s, craftsmen in the various Germanic states produced crude precursors of the two-dimensional, or "flat," military figures that were to dominate the German toy soldier market well into the 19th century. These early tin soldiers were an outgrowth of a flourishing minor industry that already had firm roots in the German states— namely, the manufacture of small lead figurines of saints and other religious symbols. It is these figures that mark the true beginning of the commercially made toy soldier.

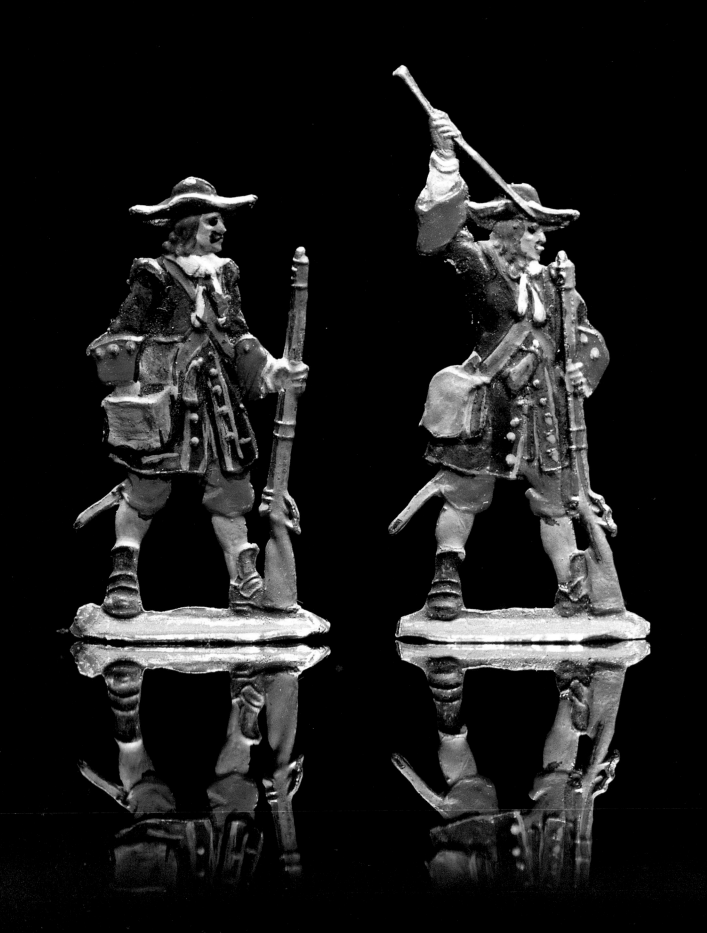

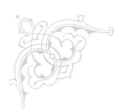

CHAPTER I
THE GERMAN MAKERS
The March of the Tin Soldiers

From the 16th century on, German pewterers and tinsmiths did a lively business fashioning miniature religious charms. Gradually, as the 18th century unfolded, these craftsmen discovered that there was a market for small-scale soldiers as well as saints. The creation of standing armies and the emergence of a succession of great military leaders such as the Duke of Marlborough, Charles XII of Sweden, and Frederick the Great of Prussia stirred national pride and furthered interest in things military.

There is ample evidence of metal toy soldiers being made in Italy, Switzerland, and Portugal in the 1700s; but it was in the German states, favored by an abundance of skilled engravers and ample supplies of lead, that the production of the tin soldiers celebrated by Hans Christian Andersen became a significant industry. Little is known about most of these early manufacturers of tin soldiers, although by the end of the 18th century many pewterers were engaged in this activity. The one exception is Johann Gottfried Hilpert, who might be called the father of the commercially made toy soldier. Son of a successful tinsmith in Coburg, Germany, Hilpert moved to Nuremberg to serve his apprenticeship and eventually set up his own business in that city.

By the early 1770s, Hilpert was mass-producing flat figures (generally defined as no more than 1 millimeter in thickness) in substantial numbers. His figures, according to one commentator, "displayed a technical and artistic ability that brought a new dimension to a crude folk art." Hilpert began with nonmilitary subjects, including miniature replicas of farm animals, theatrical performers, and other civilian scenes. But with the campaigns of Frederick the Great still fresh in the public's conscious-

ness, it was not long before military models were being produced. Indeed, the first, and most famous, of his military miniatures was a 150-millimeter portrait figure of Frederick the Great himself. Two versions of this figure, one signed "J.H., 1777" (in the Bavarian National Museum) and the other simply "H," have survived.

Hilpert subsequently produced an entire range of 2- to 3-inch toy soldiers of the various regiments of Frederick's army, to which were added figures representing the troops of other nations, particularly France and Russia. So began the parade of the *zinnfiguren*, or tin soldiers, and it was not long before other manufacturers picked up the cadence. From Nuremberg the industry spread through Germany—to Leipzig, Fürth, and Berlin. By the end of the 18th century, two-dimensional tin soldiers were being produced throughout Europe.

But it was in Germany that tin soldier making reached the heights, both in artistic quality and in production. In Nuremberg, Christian Schweiger and Johann Wolfgang Ammon followed the trail blazed by Hilpert; in Fürth, which eventually outstripped Nuremberg as the leading producer of *zinnfiguren*, the names of J. G. Lorenz and Johann Christian Allgeyer appeared on labels adorning the oval-shaped wooden boxes in which the figures were packed.

The molds used to produce flats were relatively simple affairs, consisting of two slabs of slate; on one of the smooth surfaces was engraved the figure's right profile, on the other the left. A hole was cut at the top so that molten tin could be poured into the mold when the two sides were clamped together. As the firms grew and their output swelled, lead was added to the tin to lessen the cost per figure and to provide a smoother flow of metal into the

German-made flat figures of French Napoleonic infantry, cavalry, and artillery.
Henry Kurtz Collection
Height: Infantry: 30 mm
Cavalry: 40 mm

Frontispiece—page 14. Two-dimensional flats like these German-made 17th-century musketeers dominated the toy soldier market for more than a century.
Henry Kurtz Collection
Height: 30 mm

Founded in 1839, the firm of Ernst Heinrichsen became the world's leading producer of flat figures, which Heinrichsen issued in chipwood boxes like the ones shown. →
Steve Balkin Collection
Height: 28 mm

A group of flat figures of Danish dragoons by a German maker.
Henry Kurtz Collection
Height: 36 mm

mold. Painting was on a mass-production basis and usually consisted of a few brushstrokes to suggest a basic uniform and facial features; sometimes only part of the figure was painted.

Early flat figures were literally sold by the pound (or a smaller portion). The tiniest boxes weighed about 2 ounces and contained approximately 35 infantry figures or a lesser number of cavalrymen. At the other end of the spectrum, hefty 1-pound boxes provided the buyer with a small army of nearly 300 infantry or about half that number of cavalry.

Flat figures dominated the toy soldier scene for nearly a century after Hilpert first began producing them. By the middle of the 19th century, German-made tin soldiers were being exported to most of the nations of Europe, as well as to the United States. It was during this period that Ernst Heinrichsen established the firm that was to become preeminent in its field. Founded in 1839, the Heinrichsen company not only outstripped its competitors by the sheer magnitude of production, but also in the variety of types and postures of its toy soldiers. Whether a child's fancy ranged back to the days of Hannibal or Alexander the Great or to contemporary conflicts such as the Indian Mutiny, the Crimean War, and the later wars between the great nations of Europe, there were Heinrichsen sets to satisfy his wants.

Heinrichsen figures were distinguished from other flat figures by their more realistic poses and more accurate uniforms. Most important, Heinrichsen produced figures in a uniform scale of 28 millimeters and with that one bold stroke imposed order on what had been chaos. As J. G. Garratt has written:

Heinrichsen completely changed the conception of the flat. No longer was it a large, colourful and extravagant model. The smaller size of his productions precluded any engraving other than the essential, and generally speaking the models are utilitarian. That is not to say that they are without charm, but it is a charm of a much lesser degree. For one thing the anatomy is better, and the riders are proportioned properly. . . .

Figures came in all positions, sometimes a number of figures being portrayed on one stand. Vast numbers of models went into each set, so that it was possible to build up complete armies with their armaments, or complete engagements, all the models being on the same scale.

So completely did the company dominate the market for two-dimensional toy soldiers, that the name Heinrichsen was virtually a synonym for flat figures until the firm closed its doors in the 1940s. Even today, dealer and auction catalogues often routinely list flat figures of unknown origin as Heinrichsens or "Heinrichsen-style." This is not at all surprising when one considers that Heinrichsen's major competitors closely imitated his figures, and that less scrupulous manufacturers blatantly pirated his designs.

The flat *zinnfigur* was the principal type of toy soldier produced until the last decades of the 19th century. Early in the 1800s, however, some German companies began to manufacture a somewhat sturdier figure that was thicker than a flat but not truly three-dimensional. Known as a semisolid, this figure represents an intermediate stage in the evolution of the three-dimensional (or fully round) figure that was to become the most popular form of toy soldier in our own century.

The impetus toward the semisolid stemmed mainly from financial considerations. In the early decades of the 19th century, tin soldier makers, troubled by the high cost of tin and following the traditional businessman's instinct for getting more for less, began to dilute their base metal with lead and antimony. A secondary consideration was that a fuller-bodied figure would be more realistic in appearance and thus would have greater appeal to youngsters. Unfortunately, as Ian McKenzie has pointed out in *Collecting Old Toy Soldiers*, "Unlike the alloys with greater tin content, a soft lead mixture does not permit high quality detail to be produced. So although semisolids have more 'body' than flats, they possess a lot less of the intricate engravings and fine definition. As toys they have two distinct advantages: a tendency to bend rather

In the two photos above, we see a German-made semisolid Swiss cavalryman. The figure is attached to the base by a spring mechanism, enabling a child to make the figure move back and forth with a flick of the finger.
Henry Kurtz Collection

Height: 70 mm

Among the finest toy soldiers were those produced by Johann
Haffner of Fürth. Here we see a superb figure of a French
Napoleonic cavalryman with detachable rider and saddle trappings.
Henry Kurtz Collection   Height: 90 mm

Semisolid toy soldiers, such as this Bavarian infantryman,
served as a transition between the flat and the fully round
figure.
Henry Kurtz Collection   Height: 55 mm

Heyde Russian Cossack fires at a Japanese infantryman.

Burtt Ehrlich Collection

Height: Infantryman: 52 mm
Cavalrymen: 65 mm

Often topical, Heyde produced figures representing both sides during the Russo-Japanese War of 1904–5.

Burtt Ehrlich Collection

Height: Infantry: 52 mm
Cavalry: 65 mm

than break and relative cheapness compared to flats."

Criticized by many as coarse hybrids, neither flat nor solid, they drew scorn in their own day from purists. A British observer at the Great Exhibition of 1851 disdainfully commented on "a very low class" of lead and tin soldiers from Germany. "They bend almost with their own weight and the colouring matter upon them stains a moist finger, and seriously injures the health if applied to the mouth." Nevertheless, at their best, especially in the smaller sizes of 30 to 40 millimeters, semisolids possess a definite charm. They are easily distinguishable from true solids in that while bulkier than flats, the legs of foot soldiers and cavalry horses are in alignment on the same plane. Cavalrymen were often detachable from their horses, and the riders were made bowlegged—as indeed real horse soldiers would have been—to better grip their mounts. Sometimes the horses were attached to bases by means of a simple spring mechanism. By flicking the horse's tail, a child could make the horse bob up and down, conveying a sense of motion.

That the semisolid achieved a measure of popularity in its own day is evident from the large numbers that poured out of the toy soldier mills of Germany and other European countries. Many of the leading manufacturers of flats, among them Ammon, Allgeyer, and Heinrichsen, expanded their lines to include semisolids, reproducing some of their two-dimensional figures in the new form, as well as creating new figures. The firm of G. Söhlke, founded in 1819, produced, in addition to the usual line of military figures and horse-drawn equipment, semiround figures depicting scenes from literary classics such as *Gulliver's Travels* and *Robinson Crusoe*.

The semisolid was a natural springboard to the three-dimensional (fully round) solid figure. Although it was the French, in the late 18th century, who produced the first commercially made solids, it was the Germans, with their more prolific output, who eventually captured the international market. Prominent among the early German toy soldier makers who made the jump from two-dimensional to three-dimensional figures was Johann Haffner of Fürth (and later Nuremberg). Beginning with flats and then semisolids, Haffner brought out a line of solid figures of exceptional quality in the 1860s, earning a medal for excellence at the Paris Toy Exposition of 1871. Most notable are the firm's representations of French and German troops of the Napoleonic Wars, the foot figures generally being 49 millimeters in size, and cavalrymen a proportional 72 millimeters.

By far the finest of the Haffners are the mounted figures. The spirited horses are well proportioned and realistically animated; both rider and saddlecloth are detachable, and the horseman comes with a seat peg that fits through a hole in the saddlecloth and the horse to secure him firmly in place when mounted. Haffner figures stand head and shoulders above most of the toy soldiers produced by the firm's contemporaries, and have been favorably compared to the finely detailed model soldiers collected by many present-day military miniature buffs.

Other manufacturers of German solids in the mid to late 19th century include Johann Carl Fraas, a Bavarian, and Conrad Schildknecht of Fürth. Georg Spenküch of Nuremberg produced both military and nonmilitary figures, including bullfights and a miniature model of the Nuremberg–Fürth railroad. Many of these manufacturers are now merely names to be found in dusty archives. In the 1870s, their little lead troops were swept aside by the mighty legions of Georg Heyde of Dresden, whose columns of toy soldiers were to march into the playrooms of children in every nation of Europe—and eventually the United States and other, more distant lands.

Often dated from the 1870s, it seems certain now that the Heyde company first got involved in the soldier trade shortly after its founding in the 1830s, and that by the 1850s, with Gustav Adolf Theodor Heyde at its head, it was well established in the business. But it was not until the early 1870s, when Georg Heyde took over the reins of the company, that the firm reached its productive peak; the rectangular, maroon-colored boxes in which Heyde figures were packed carry reproductions of medals won at various toy fairs and expositions in 1877, 1879, and 1881.

While Bismarck's Prussian armies waged a series of successful wars against Denmark, Austria, and France—

Prussian Guard artillery on the march.
Burtt Ehrlich Collection

Height: Foot figures: 52 mm
Mounted: 65 mm

A close-up of a Heyde Prussian Lancer.
Burtt Ehrlich Collection

Height: 65 mm

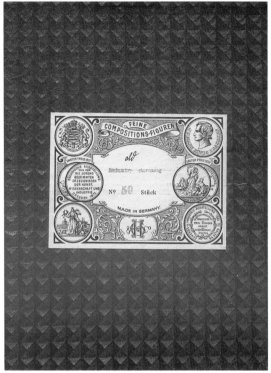

Heyde figures came in maroon-colored rectangular boxes bearing a simple label that displayed medals won by the firm at various expositions.
Burtt Ehrlich Collection

A set of Heyde infantry of Frederick the Great, a period that received considerable attention from the firm.
Burtt Ehrlich Collection   Height: 52 mm

Heyde's toy soldiers came in a range of sizes from 43 mm to 145 mm.
Here we see a group of 75mm Black Watch Highlanders.
Burtt Ehrlich Collection   Height: 75 mm

culminating in the humiliating defeat of the French at Sedan in 1870—Heyde's toy armies won commercial victories of their own over European competitors. The secret of success was simple: produce bigger, better, and more elaborate sets of toy soldiers than anyone else. Unlike the lead troops of other companies, whose figures came in a few basic poses, Heyde figures did everything but walk and talk. As Peter Johnson observes in *Toy Armies*: "No other maker has produced figures in such a variety of poses.... His troops do more than march, stand guard, shoot and charge. They bivouac with mugs of coffee and bottles of schnapps, climb trees and chop wood, light fires, tend cooking pots, towel themselves, play cards, hang out washing, study maps, uncoil wire, sweep decks, carry shells, feed horses, sleep, fall wounded and lie dead."

Surely that was enough activity to satisfy the creative play fantasies of even the most precocious child. Making this possible was the use of a soft metal alloy, pliable enough so that skillful animators could twist and contort arms, legs, and torsos into virtually every conceivable position. Heads were separately cast, usually with greater tin content to better show facial detail, and then plugged into the bodies. Other casters produced weapons, flags, and all manner of implements to be soldered to hands and bodies as required. Figures came in many sizes, with the smallest infantryman just under 2 inches (43 mm) and the tallest mounted cavalry trooper rising to nearly 6 inches (145 mm). Larger figures (and sometimes smaller ones) came with removable helmets and with swords and bayonets that slipped out of scabbards. Given below are the various sizes as stated in an early 1920s Heyde catalogue.

Figure type		Size of figure
		(in millimeters)
Cavalry, fine massive figures, on horseback,	size 3	48
	size 2	65
	size 1	78
	size 00	90
	size 0	115
	size 0^I	120
	size 0^{II}	145
Infantry, fine massive figures,	size 3	43
	size 2	52
	size 1	58
	size 00	68
	size 0	75
	size 0^I	87
	size 0^{II}	120
Cavalry, massive, 2nd quality	size 2b	58
Infantry	size 2b	48
Cavalry, 2nd quality, extra large	size 1c	65
Infantry	size 1c	55
Cavalry, massive, 2nd quality	size 3b	55
Infantry	size 3b	40

Heyde's post–World War I catalogues listed some 1,400 different sets, but this was merely the tip of the iceberg, indicating what was readily available rather than the company's capability of filling specific demands. Unlike the catalogues of Britains, for example, in which reference numbers were assigned to sets representing specific regiments or national units, Heyde's catalogue numbers, for the most part, merely described a type of set and its contents. So one would learn that Number 170 contained 21 Size 2 (52mm) infantrymen "in 3 different positions: shooting kneeling, upright standing, and stretched out [prone]," while Number 176 offered the buyer an assortment of 40 infantrymen representing four different regiments. By the simple expedient of plugging in a different head and painting on appropriate uniform colors, a standard infantry figure could be transformed into a soldier of virtually any nation in the world.

As Heyde catalogues informed prospective retailers, they had only to specify the type of figures required and the company would see to it that the troops were decked out in the proper uniforms. Size 2 figures were the most commonly exported, the larger sizes being generally pre-

Heyde followed the First World War with no hard feelings making
troops of the Western Allies. Here is a set of British Troops in steel
helmets with their distinctive lozenge shaped tanks, and their
original box.
London Toy Museum Collection   Figures height: 48 mm

A large-size Heyde Grenadier Guard dwarfs his Britains counterpart,
a Royal Welch Fusilier.
Burtt Ehrlich Collection Height: Heyde figure: 110 mm (also on cover)
                                        Britains figure: 54 mm

27

An Indian warrior carries off a woman captive in this Wild West vignette by Heyde.
Burtt Ehrlich Collection   Height: 65 mm

Georg Heyde's toy soldiers were known for their active poses, as is evident in this scene of an American Indian encampment.
Burtt Ehrlich Collection   Height: 52 mm

A Turkish sultan crosses the desert on his elaborately adorned camel in this group by Heyde.
Burtt Ehrlich Collection
Height: Camel: 75 mm
Foot: 52 mm

Heyde was known for its unusual display sets, such as this Turkish caravan.
Burtt Ehrlich Collection
Height: Camel: 75 mm
Mounted: 65 mm
Foot: 52 mm

ferred at home, and these could be supplied "in the uniforms of whatever military organized nation of the world." However, the firm was willing "to satisfy any justified requirement of our customers as regards soldiers manufactured in all other sizes." If the retailer was uncertain about his needs, Heyde, like a good doctor, would happily prescribe the proper cure for the lead soldier cravings of his youthful customers, delivering "assortments which we, on account of our experience . . . think fittest for the market of the country of destination."

But it was more than mere catering to national pride that accounted for the firm's success. Above all, it was the dazzling array of special sets, from Roman armies on the march to hand-to-hand combat in battles of the Franco–Prussian War. Included were American Indian encampments, grand reviews, coronation scenes, lion and tiger hunts, Arab caravans, and polar expeditions. Even the set titles were enticing. How easy to succumb to the allure of Set Number 58, "Kettledrum-Car of the Electorate of Saxony, of the time of about 1760, drawn by four horses," which, in its most elaborate form, included four mounted trumpeters along with three bagpipers and three hautboyists, and two grooms on foot, all "finely painted in subdued colors"; or Set Number 1069, described in the catalogue as "Distress landing of aeroplane in the Afghan Desert, with painted ground in desert style," which, in addition to the plane, contained 10 different figures on horseback and 11 others on foot.

Writing in the *Old Toy Soldier Newsletter*, Lee Daniels recalls being given a Heyde horse-drawn military transport set as a Christmas present in the early 1920s. "The figures were in khaki with broad-brimmed campaign hats on the marching escort, and billed garrison hats on the seated wagon drivers, each of which held a long, curved whip. There must have been six to eight wagons, including an open forage wagon, canvas-covered supply wagons, and one interesting sheet metal officers' van with a back door that really opened. . . . Each wagon was made of sheet metal cleverly soldered at the corners, and attached [to these] were fixed cast wheels, all of

equal size. Pulling each wagon was a team of horses soldered together on a sheet metal base and hooked to the wagon pole."

Heyde produced a marvelous range of historical sets, beginning with the ancient armies of Rome, Greece, and Macedonia, and including also Egyptians, Persians, and early Germanic warriors, the latter costumed as if in a Wagnerian opera, with wolfskin garments and horned helmets. Special displays of ancient warriors were particularly impressive. One depicted the Sack of Troy, complete with a facsimile of the walled city, temple structures, Achilles in his chariot dragging behind him the vanquished Hector, and a variety of Greek and Trojan soldiers and civilians. The glory of Rome received full tribute in "The Triumphal March of Germanicus," in which Germanicus Caesar, son of the famous general Nero Claudius Drusus, seated in the mahout of a gaily bedecked elephant, led his victorious legions along a banner-lined Appian Way.

Then came Norman knights and Saracen warriors, ready to reenact the Holy Crusades; medieval knights were abundant and were featured in special display sets such as "The Battle of the Knights" and "The Excursion of Robber Knights." The periods of Frederick the Great and the American Revolution comprised an important part of the Heyde catalogue. Prominent were sets of "Der Alte Fritz" and his generals, of the triumphal parade of enemy battle flags captured at the Battle of Hohenfriedberg, and of a magnificent encampment of Frederick the Great's army, with officers seated at a table drinking from oversized goblets, and soldiers resting on straw mats, cooking over fires, grooming horses, and performing all sorts of chores. The same set, slightly reworked, was easily transformed into "A Bivouac During the American War of Independence." Other troops of the American Revolutionary War included Washington's Life Guard mounted at the gallop, light dragoons and light infantry, soldiers of the Pennsylvania Line, and buckskin-clad sharpshooters.

Heyde's historical range featured equestrian personality figures, many in the larger sizes of 90 to 145 mil-

American Continentals and British
Grenadiers by Heyde.
Burtt Ehrlich Collection
Height: Foot figures: 52 mm
Mounted: 65 mm

Heyde issued horse-drawn transport to
support its toy troops. The wagons
were made of tinplate with cast-lead
wheels.
Burtt Ehrlich Collection
Height: Mounted: 65 mm

Many toy soldier companies produced models of the State Coach of
England, but the Heyde version was by far the most exquisitely
detailed.
Burtt Ehrlich Collection   Height: 52 mm

A troop of French cuirassiers by Heyde trots across a parade
ground.
Burtt Ehrlich Collection   Height: 65 mm

limeters. The catalogue listed obvious choices, such as George Washington, Frederick the Great, and Lord Kitchener, with others provided on demand. Attentive to the royal households of Europe, Heyde provided appropriate figures of Kings Edward VII and George V of England, Kaiser Wilhelm, and others. Set Number 44 was a splendid replica of the State Coach of England drawn by eight horses, which, with its excellent detail, was probably the finest toy model of this coach ever made.

Firmly established by the end of the 1870s as Germany's leading toy soldier maker, Heyde quickly found new worlds to conquer. Great Britain proved a ready outlet for the firm's products, for until the 1890s there were no competing English companies. Ever mindful of British pride in their empire and the small but well-disciplined regular army that defended it, Heyde's factory turned out a multitude of British Army sets, from massive "Parade" displays with more than 100 cavalry and infantry, including a band and horse-drawn artillery teams, to pith-helmeted Camel Corpsmen equipped for action in the Sudan campaigns of the 1880s and 1890s. Colonial forces were represented by Gurkhas and Sikhs, and a most popular Indian Army Elephant Battery with an elephant-drawn field gun and various gunners and outriders. The American market was similarly well exploited, with Civil War and Spanish-American War troops following hard on the heels of the American Revolutionary War series.

Always topical, Heyde kept abreast of current conflicts, issuing sets that permitted graphic reenactments of battles fought in the major wars and military campaigns from the latter part of the 19th century to World War I. Earliest among these were "Battle" sets of the Franco–Prussian War, with either fully round or semisolid figures—the largest including buildings and other scenic backdrops. "The realism of war was very much evident [in these sets]," notes one authority. "All the soldiers except the dead and wounded were in fighting positions and there was a liberal supply of bushes, trees, hedges and fences. One set included a farmhouse, a windmill, and a signpost [all semiround]. On one stand an officer of one

army gripped a colour held by one of his foes. On another base a soldier, standing by a tree, was shooting a mounted officer of the enemy."

In due course, the Boer War was dealt with. The personnel in standard marching and action sets were dressed either in the khaki service uniforms that had by then been adopted by the British Army, or in the more nondescript uniforms of the Dutch farmer-guerrillas who opposed them. The sets also included various support units such as pontoon wagons, supply trains, artillery teams, and horse-drawn ambulances. Later came miniature models of the forces participating in the Russo–Japanese War, the Balkan conflicts, and the bitter trench fighting of the "Great War" of 1914–18.

Heyde was especially noted for its military bands. Cavalry bands came with 6 to 12 musicians mounted on standing or walking horses and could be had in any of five sizes, from 58 to 115 millimeters. Infantry bands came in boxes of 10 to 30 pieces—offering a greater variety of instruments than those of most other toy soldier makers—in a range of sizes comparable to the mounted bands. A bandmaster with baton replaced the more common drum major with staff. Unquestionably, the masterpiece of Heyde's repertoire of miniature musicians was its "Music Box" bandstand, with conductor, bandsmen at attention, and music stands. Inside the bandstand was a clockwork mechanism that when wound with a key, played the national anthem or other patriotic song of a particular nation and also caused the baton arm of the bandmaster to move up and down in a conducting motion. The "Music Box" bandstand was available in three sizes: 52 millimeters (Size 2), 68 millimeters (Size 00), and 75 millimeters (Size 0).

A seated military band, with 20 musicians and 10 music stands, was produced in the 52-millimeter scale. There were also two seated civilian bands, one called "Jazz Band," whose musicians played various percussion instruments, and the other a 17-piece "Darkie Jazz Band." Musicians and chairs were cast as single pieces, accompanied by separate music stands. All of these sets

Heyde did a lively export business to Great Britain, producing many
special sets such as this Royal Artillery Mountain Battery.
Burtt Ehrlich Collection   Height: 52 mm

Heyde committed the unpardonable sin of putting some of its British
Life Guards and Royal Horse Guards (shown above) on brown
horses instead of regulation black.
Burtt Ehrlich Collection   Height: 65 mm

A mixed group of late-19th-century
American military types by Heyde.
Burtt Ehrlich Collection
Height: Foot figures: 52 mm
Mounted figure: 65 mm

French Chasseurs à Cheval, 1914, in
their original Heyde box.
Burtt Ehrlich Collection   Height: 65 mm

are now extremely rare items.

In the years after World War I, as "Lucky Lindbergh" winged his way across the Atlantic and the public thrilled to the exploits of other equally daring aviators, Heyde kept up with the changing times. The coming of the air age was saluted by a full-scale "Aerial Port" that featured two monoplanes, an airport terminal and a control tower with a battery-operated searchlight, as well as passengers, airport personnel, runway flag markers, and scenic props. Military aviation was represented in Set Number 737, "Aeronaute Troops," comprising a zeppelin—charmingly described in German-English as "1 balloon mit spring motion"—a 17-man ground crew, cyclists, and a mounted officer. Not surprisingly, given the early development of airships in Germany, zeppelins were prominent in other sets, including Number 1014, which consisted of an electrically driven and lighted zeppelin "with special motor for continuous and shuttle current."

Heyde's extensive civilian output included circus, zoo, and railway scenes, bullfights, a miniature playground for children, and various hunt scenes, among them a winter hunt that, with its snow-covered fir trees, hedges, and bridges, quite realistically conveyed a sense of a frigid forest winter wonderland. Ever-popular cowboys and Indians appeared in a series of "Buffalo Bill" sets—with the American folk hero either hunting buffalo or saving stagecoaches and settlements from Indian attacks—and one of cowboys breaking wild horses. There were also sets depicting the birth of Jesus Christ and the adventures of Robinson Crusoe.

Often faulted for their anatomical shortcomings, Heyde figures, particularly in the smaller sizes, do have a somewhat awkward look, with short, stumpy legs attached to oversized torsos, and rounded elbows resulting from the hasty twisting of arms into various positions by the animators. What purists lose sight of, however, is that, above all, Heyde figures were meant to be toys and not precisely sculpted replicas. Lee Daniels, a long-time Heyde collector, pays tribute to the toylike charm of Heydes when he observes that they "resembled the illustrations in my copy of Robert Louis Stevenson's *A Child's Garden of Verses*, which had soldiers filling the pages next to 'The Land of Counterpane,' and 'The Dumb Soldier.'"

Unfortunately, positive identification of Heyde's models presents a major problem for collectors. No identifying markings were placed underneath the bases; and unless the figures come in their original boxes, or their provenance is clearly known, it is hard to separate Heydes from the toy soldiers of other contemporary German makers—not to mention the horde of pirate firms that unashamedly reproduced Heyde designs under their own labels. Only recently was it discovered that many toy soldiers thought to be Heydes were in actuality the work of Gebrüder Heinrich of Fürth. So closely do Heinrich figures resemble Heydes that, as one commentator put it, "the only sure way [of telling the difference] is to have the figures in their original boxes."

Heinrich's toy troops were usually packed in wooden boxes topped by a sliding lid panel. The firm appears to have exported large numbers of its figures to Great Britain; and its trademark, a mounted knight carrying a banner with the letters "GH" over the horse's head, was registered in that country in 1895. Sets intended for the British market were packaged in boxes bearing a four-color label with the heading "The British Army" and with full-size illustrations of British soldiers and sailors, including a Grenadier Guard, a Gordon Highlander, an 11th Hussar, and a State Trumpeter playing his instrument.

Despite the difficulties in distinguishing real Heydes from the products of imitators, some specific characteristics of the most common Size 2 figures are a useful guide. Heyde infantrymen on parade always step off on the right foot, never the left; their necks are thinner than those of other German makers; bases for infantrymen are usually $\frac{3}{4}$ inch long and $\frac{1}{2}$ inch wide (those of competitors are often larger); and the field equipment, molded onto the figures, is always of German pattern and not that of other national armies being represented. (It has been stated in some sources that Heyde infantrymen invariably carry their

French infantry, 1914, in parade uniforms,
still stitched in their original Heyde box.
Burtt Ehrlich Collection   Height: 52 mm

A detachment of Prussian Lancers by Heyde passes in review.
Burtt Ehrlich Collection   Height: 65 mm

Band of the Life Guards by Heyde in its original box.
Burtt Ehrlich Collection   Height: 65 mm

A close-up of a World War I British cavalryman by Heyde.
Burtt Ehrlich Collection   Height: 65 mm

rifles on the right shoulder but, as many existing sets bear out, this is simply not so.) Identifying features of cavalrymen include a seat peg between the legs of the rider that, when inserted into a hole in the top of the horse, keeps him firmly in the saddle; and what one writer refers to as "the comical belly-to-ground charging horse." A curiosity of the Size 2 cavalry figures is that while the riders were fully round, the horses were frequently semiround. (As a rule, trotting horses were of the thin variety, while those galloping and at the halt were full-bodied.)

Early Heyde figures—those produced before World War I—are widely regarded as superior in quality to models issued between the two world wars. L. W. Richards speculates that an entirely new set of molds may have been produced in the 1920s. This would account for the fact that postwar Size 2 figures did not strictly adhere to the 52-millimeter scale, as stated in the catalogues, but were slightly smaller, varying from 47 to 50 millimeters. Such a reduction, multiplied by the millions of toy soldiers turned out by the firm's Dresden factory, would have resulted in a considerable saving in metal costs at a time of severe economic hardship in Germany. Nevertheless, until the very end, the firm's little metal men retained the exuberant character that made the name Heyde a synonym for fine toy soldiers during its seventy-odd years of production.

At the beginning of this century, a new type of toy soldier was introduced in Germany by Otto and Max Hausser. Under the Elastolin trademark the Hausser brothers manufactured composition figures made of a mixture of sawdust, kaolin, bone glue, and other ingredients. When compressed and applied to a wire skeleton, the result was a plasterlike figure. Early models were rather large, 10 to 14 centimeters, while later figures were generally 54 to 60 millimeters. Although it is beyond the scope of this book to treat in detail the subject of composition figures, it is worth noting that the company produced an extensive line of military models, tinplate vehicles, cannons and other equipment, a popular "Wild West" series with stagecoaches and covered wagons, a

"Prince Valiant" series of medieval types, and some farm, zoo, and circus figures, all of which are fully discussed in Reggie Polaine's fine book *The War Toys*. Elastolin figures are easily identifiable by their thick oval bases, which carry the mark "Elastolin" or "Elastolin/Germany" in the hollowed-out underside.

Two other composition figure makers, the firms of Lineol and Leyla, started up in the 1930s, with Lineol being the superior of the two in quality of product. During the Nazi era, all of the composition toy soldier manufacturers turned their attention to the glorification of the armed forces and political personalities of the Third Reich and its Fascist allies. Goose-stepping German troops paraded out of the factories, accompanied by brown-shirted SA and black-uniformed SS contingents. Added touches of realism were provided by rifles firing explosive caps and movable right arms on models of Hitler, Goebbels, and other Nazi leaders that sprang up to give the Fascist salute. As part of the Nazi propaganda effort, substantial numbers of these toys were shipped abroad, and at least one American collector is known to have had his Lineol collection of German Army troops confiscated by FBI agents shortly after America's entry into the war.

Among the major German toy soldier manufacturers, only Elastolin pulled itself out of the bombed-out ruins of postwar Germany to flourish again. Some composition figures were reissued after the war, but for the most part, the firm concentrated, until its recent closing, on expanding and improving an excellent line of well-detailed plastic figures begun in the 1940s. In the case of the greatest of all the German toy soldier companies, Georg Heyde of Dresden, the story ends on a grim note. Allied bombers swept over Dresden in February 1945, unleashing a devastating aerial attack that left the city, and the Heyde factory on Alaunstrasse, a pile of charred rubble. Heyde's molds and the company's records were destroyed and no effort was made to revive the firm after the war.

For Heyde collectors, all that remains are nostalgic

In a confrontation reminiscent of the Battle of Rorke's Drift, British infantrymen by Heyde beat off an attack by fierce Britains Zulus.
Burtt Ehrlich Collection

Height: Heydes: 50 mm
Britains: 54 mm

A Heyde "Music Box" bandstand with a British Guards band. When the clockwork mechanism in the bandstand was wound, it played an appropriate national tune and also caused the bandmaster's conducting arm to move up and down.

Burtt Ehrlich Collection   Height: 52 mm

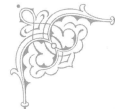

An extremely rare large-size Heyde Band of the Prussian Garde du Corps, an elite military unit.
Burtt Ehrlich Collection   Height: 75 mm

Prussian bandsmen perform in concert in this detail shot of the Garde du Corps band.
Burtt Ehrlich Collection   Height: 75 mm

memories of halcyon days when Heyde sets were to be found in major department stores in all parts of the globe. Some American collectors from the Chicago area wistfully recall a time before World War II when an entire sales counter at Marshall Field's department store overflowed with lavish Heyde display sets. Even a youngster whose parents could not afford the $8 or more for a complete set might still come away with a 50-cent figure carefully selected from a display of individual pieces salvaged from damaged sets. Speaking for many, an American collector, looking back on those golden prewar days, exclaimed: "Oh, to be back at the Heyde counter of Field's of the past era, with the 1928 prices and the wide variety of sets, but with my credit cards and charge plates of today!"

A monoplane comes in for a landing at a Heyde airport, while passengers prepare to board another plane being prepared for takeoff by ground crewmen.
Burtt Ehrlich Collection

A group of Chinese Boxers by Heyde.
Burtt Ehrlich Collection   Height: 52 mm

This magnificent Indian maharaja's ceremonial
elephant is a fine example of the nonmilitary
figures produced by Heyde.
Burtt Ehrlich Collection   Height: Riders: 52 mm
                                        Elephant: 120 mm

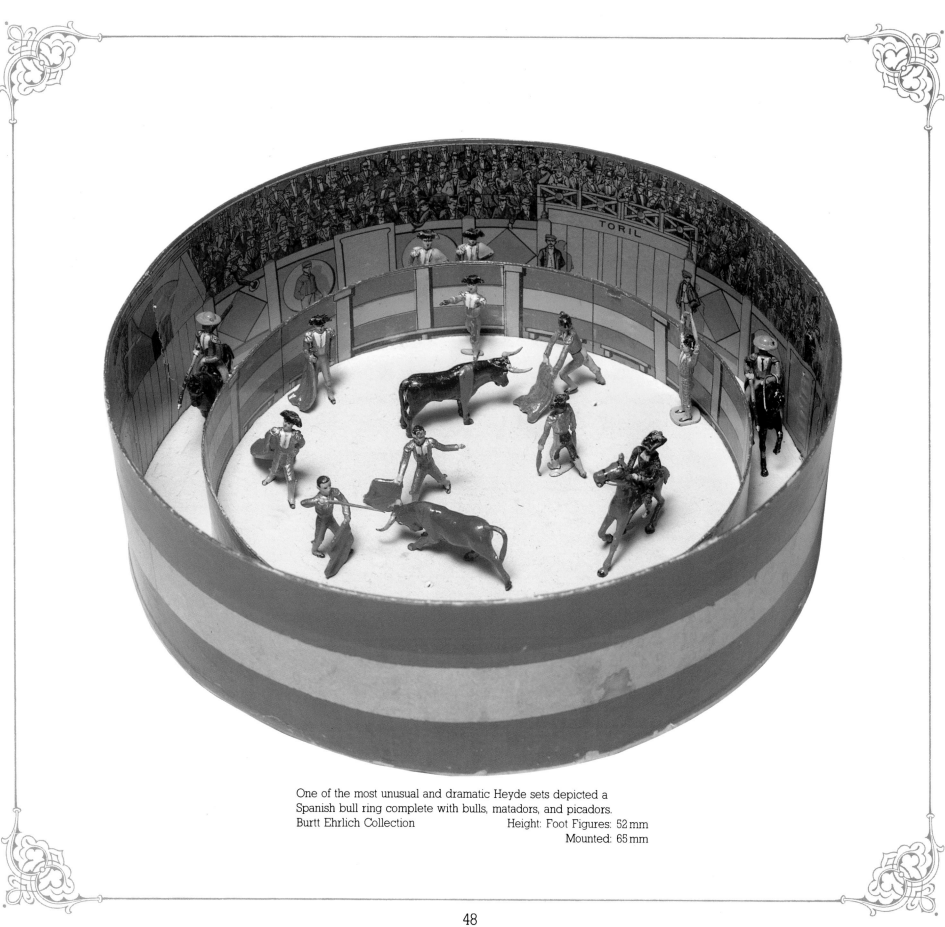

One of the most unusual and dramatic Heyde sets depicted a
Spanish bull ring complete with bulls, matadors, and picadors.
Burtt Ehrlich Collection   Height: Foot Figures: 52 mm
                                           Mounted: 65 mm

A Heinrich box lid with a label used on sets exported to Great
Britain and other European countries.
Burtt Ehrlich Collection   Height: Box lid: 165 mm × 250 mm

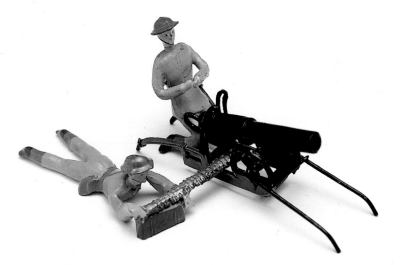

← Large-size British line infantrymen by Heinrich, one of Heyde's
principal German rivals.
Burtt Ehrlich Collection

A Heinrich British World War I machine-gun unit in action.
Burtt Ehrlich Collection   Height: Prone figure: 55 mm
                                    Kneeling figure: 35 mm
                                    Length of gun: 60 mm

CHAPTER II

THE FRENCH MAKERS
A Solid Line of Troops

The year was 1792. France had been set aflame by the torch of revolution, and through the streets of Paris marched mobs of peasants armed with pikes, axes, swords, and muskets, singing their new hymn of liberty, "La Marseillaise." On August 10, a mob led by troops of the National Guard stormed the Tuileries Palace of Louis XVI. The king had already fled to safety, but his loyal Swiss Guards fought to defend the palace until Louis sent word that they were not to fire on the rampaging peasants. The Swiss troops obeyed and were slaughtered to the last man. From the window of a nearby building, an obscure but ambitious artillery officer named Napoleon Bonaparte watched as the swirling mass of farmers and artisans swarmed across the palace grounds and struck the blow that toppled the French monarchy.

In a quiet corner of Paris, far away from the brittle sound of musketry and the crowds shouting their revolutionary slogans, a French craftsman named Lucotte was quietly making a minor revolution of his own. For it was in the Lucotte workshop, while the Germans were still turning out their fragile flats, that the first successful line of commercially made, solid toy soldiers was produced. The three-dimensional figures of Lucotte were indeed revolutionary in that era of the thin tin soldier, and they established a trend that would reach full fruition in the later figures of Mignot, Haffner, and Heyde.

The exact date that Lucotte began producing his *ronde-bosse* (fully round) lead soldiers cannot be pinpointed. A French source states that the Lucotte factory was "founded before 1789," but provides no supporting evidence. C. B. G. Mignot, the firm that subsequently absorbed Lucotte, has traditionally claimed that as a result of the merger, it could rightly trace its own beginnings "to

the old trademark LC [Lucotte], whose molds date from the time of the French Revolution."

It seems probable, therefore, that Lucotte began manufacturing his toy troops around the time the Bastille was stormed. In the years that followed, as France became, in the words of one historian, "an armed camp and a vast munitions factory," Lucotte produced figures that caught the martial spirit of the day. Beginning with French Revolutionary troops, in their jaunty cocked hats and striped trousers, he kept pace with Napoleon's rise to power by fashioning miniature representations of the brilliantly garbed regiments of the First Empire's Grande Armée. Stalwart grenadiers of the Imperial Guard, in their towering bearskins, took their place alongside battalions of chasseurs, voltigeurs, sappeurs, and line infantry.

Cavalrymen, too, trooped forth in squadrons from the Lucotte molds. Hussars, the peacocks of the mounted arm, with their distinctive pelisses draped over their shoulders, helmeted dragoons and cuirassiers, lancers and carabiniers, all splendidly mounted. There were horse-drawn artillery teams, field forges, and kitchens, as well as mounted and foot bands to play the troops into battle. One of the most splendid of Lucotte's creations was a group of portrait figures of Napoleon and his generals, each resplendent in his distinctive uniform and mounted on a horse with appropriate trappings. There is Marshal Ney in green tunic, wearing a lancer-style cap and carrying his marshal's baton in his right hand, his horse draped in a saddlecloth made from a tiger's skin—complete with the beast's head; and Eugène de Beauharnais, stepson of Napoleon by his marriage to Joséphine, fur-trimmed pelisse dangling from his left shoulder, his uniform dripping with gold lace.

← Magnificently uniformed French hussars and dragoons of Napoleon's Grande Armée parade through the streets of Paris.
Burtt Ehrlich Collection
Height: 75 mm

At the time of the French Revolution, a Parisian craftsman named Lucotte began manufacturing the first commercial line of three-dimensional toy soldiers. His focus was on French Revolutionary and Napoleonic troops, which included the mounted staff officers shown above.
Burtt Ehrlich Collection   Height: 77 mm

A column of Napoleon's Imperial Guard Grenadiers, one of the many units of the Grande Armée turned out by Lucotte. Note the long stride of the soldiers, a characteristic of Lucotte figures.
Burtt Ehrlich Collection   Height: 60 mm

When C. B. G. Mignot took over the Lucotte operation, it continued to issue a selection of figures made from original Lucotte molds, including such choice items as Napoleon and his general staff. This set continued to appear in Mignot catalogues and those of its principal retail outlet in Paris, Au Plat d'Etain, well into the 1930s. Officially designated "Le Grand Etat-Major," it was described in the catalogues as "25 portrait figures, superfine painting, in a luxurious box." Its cost in the 1930s was 600 francs (nearly $20 according to the prewar value of the franc)—a price suggesting that it was intended more for the adult collector than for children. Recently, Mignot reissued 12 of the figures, individually boxed, in a limited edition of 100 sets. Although prohibitively priced even by today's standards, it is likely that the series will become a collector's item in its own right.

Lucotte figures are easily distinguishable from the later toy soldiers of C. B. G. Mignot. Infantry march with longer strides, their legs bent in more naturalistic fashion, while Mignot infantrymen have a shorter, somewhat stiff-legged gait. Bases for Lucotte foot figures are generally longer than those of their Mignot counterparts. Cavalry figures also exhibit marked differences. Lucotte horses are slimmer and more elegant in appearance, both rider and saddle trappings are detachable, and the reins are movable. Mignot's horse soldiers are also detachable, but the reins and saddles are molded onto the horse, not separately cast, and the horses' tails are shorter than those of Lucotte mounts. Finally, there is the distinct Lucotte emblem. Caught up in the Napoleonic frenzy, Lucotte adopted as his trademark the "Imperial Bee" of Bonaparte, with the letters "L" and "C" standing sentrylike on either side of the bee.

Lucotte continued to produce its line independently until the early decades of the 19th century; it was eventually taken over by the firm that evolved into C. B. G. Mignot. Here the record becomes murky. What is known is that in 1825 three entrepreneurs named Cuperly, Blondel, and Gerbeau established a toy company—a fact recorded in *Bazar Parisien*, a contemporary trade journal—and that in 1838 the firm began using "C. B. G." as its trademark. At what point the name Mignot was added to the list, or exactly when the Lucotte operation came under C. B. G.'s wing is unclear, since even the company is unable to provide concrete details. Based on a few fragments of information, several writers have claimed that Lucotte was taken over by C. B. G. at some point in the 1820s or 1830s, and that C. B. G.–Lucotte, in turn, was gobbled up by Mignot in the 1870s. A more romantic variation has a Mignot marrying into the Lucotte family—in the traditional European manner of forging alliances between rival dynasties—and thus acquiring title to the valuable Lucotte molds.

However, Professor George Keester, author of *Soldats de Plomb*, a study of Mignot's pre–World War I production, maintains that Henri Mignot joined C. B. G. around 1900, by which time a member of the Gerbeau family was sole owner of the firm. The company then became known as Gerbeau and Mignot, and subsequently Mignot (C. B. G.), although today it is simply known as Mignot. Meanwhile, the Lucotte line had apparently continued independently (or possibly under the wing of C. B. G. or another company), with new figures in the Lucotte style being designed and added to the list as late as World War I. According to Professor Keester, it was not until 1928 that the Lucotte molds were formally incorporated into the Mignot operation.

By that time, C. B. G. Mignot had been producing its own line of toy soldiers for more than a century. Nor was it the only French company turning out three-dimensional solid toy soldiers in the 1800s. From its earliest days, C. B. G. faced competition from other Parisian firms. Records indicate that two such companies, both located on the Rue Grénatat, were functioning in the mid-1820s. One, the firm of Leveille, was producing "soldiers on horse and on foot" along with tin toys and dollhouses, while a few doors down the street a gentleman named Delacroix offered "soldiers of all kinds." To these were added the names of Lemoyne and Tessiere, Fessard, Rigaud, Ringel, and Trousset and Laumonier in the years

In this close-up of a group of French cuirassiers, we see some of the characteristics of Lucotte figures: the more elegant-looking horses, movable reins, and superior sculpting of the cavalrymen.
Burtt Ehrlich Collection

Height: 77 mm

Gaily garbed Napoleonic bandsman by Lucotte.
Burtt Ehrlich Collection

Height: 60 mm

This Lucotte model of a horse-drawn Napoleonic ambulance
duplicated an actual mobile surgical unit developed for quick
movement on the battlefield.
Burtt Ehrlich Collection   Height: Mounted figures: 75 mm

58

Lucotte continued to produce
its own line of toy soldiers
until the early part of the 20th
century, when these Japanese
infantrymen were turned out.
Burtt Ehrlich Collection
Height: 55 mm

Although Mignot is best
known for its premier line
of 55mm figures, it also issued
smaller semiround figures in
32mm and 40mm scale.
This impressive diorama shows
medieval troops storming
a castle. A grisly touch is
the gentleman hanging from
the gallows on the left side
of the picture.
Burtt Ehrlich Collection
Height: 32 mm

between 1830 and 1880.

None of these firms achieved any standing comparable to that enjoyed by C. B. G. Mignot, as is evidenced by the fact that their names and the toy troops they manufactured are virtually unknown to today's collectors. Mignot stood head and shoulders above the rest in France, just as Heyde of Dresden, its leading foreign competitor, did in Germany. By the 1850s, Mignot was generally recognized as France's premier producer of *soldats de plomb* (lead soldiers), a position that has never been seriously challenged. By that time also, Mignot figures were being exported to other countries. Some of them apparently found their way to the United States. An 1860s photograph shows President Lincoln and his son Tad playing with toy soldiers that are almost certainly Mignots. (However, it is not known whether these figures belonged to the Lincolns or were props provided by the photographer.)

Since Mignot figures are universally regarded as toy soldiers of the finest quality, it is worthwhile to examine the company's various lines in some detail. Mignot produced fully round figures of 55 millimeters (75 mm for cavalry), smaller semirounds ranging in size from 32 to 50 millimeters, cheaper-grade hollow-cast figures of 50 to 80 millimeters, and later a series of unbreakable figures in aluminum. They even issued an outstanding line of flats in the 1930s. However, because their premier line of 55-millimeter solid figures of lead alloy—designated figures of the *troisième grandeur* (third size) in their catalogues— commands the most attention from serious collectors, our focus shall be on this type.

Predictably, Mignot concentrated on soldiers of France, both historical and contemporary. Battalions of French infantry and cavalry of the Napoleonic Wars marched across playroom floors to refight the battles of Marengo, Austerlitz, and Jena. Particularly impressive were the cavalry units, which included the famed Polish Lancers, Mamelukes, Grenadiers à Cheval of the Imperial Guard, and assorted dragoons, hussars, and cuirassiers. Less numerous were the fighting men of those nations allied against Napoleon; and an English observer,

perhaps ungenerously, has suggested that Mignot grudgingly produced foreign troops solely to provide French tots with cannon fodder for the ever-victorious French Army. Nevertheless, there were some creditable representations of Prussian, Austrian, and Russian troops, including splendid sets of Prussian hussars in their black and silver uniforms and Russian Cossacks in flaming red coats and black fur hats. British troops fared less well at the hands of Mignot's master modellers—perhaps because they had been a mite too successful at Waterloo. The red-coated line infantry and Scottish Highlanders are not as carefully designed as their French counterparts and do not project the sturdy toughness that prompted the Duke of Wellington to say to his army, "I do not know what effect they will have upon the enemy, but they certainly frighten me."

When French children tired of refighting the wars of Napoleon, they could move on to the Crimean War, the colonial wars of North Africa and Indochina, and World War I, which received the most coverage after the Napoleonic period. As France's empire expanded into the broiling deserts of North Africa and the rice paddies of Southeast Asia, Mignot followed the flag. French troops included the Colonial Infantry in white pith helmets, blue tunics, and white trousers, and the well-known Zouaves in their distinctive short blue jackets trimmed in red, baggy red pants tucked into white gaiters, and turban-and-fez headgear. Naturally, the celebrated French Foreign Legion was represented by several sets.

Native troops who fought alongside the French in their colonial wars of conquest also abound. There are colorfully robed Spahis (North African cavalry), Goumiers (guides), Turcos, and Senegalese. Troops and warriors from the exotic lands the French invaded include Dahomeans, Tonkinese, Annamites, and Moroccans. An interesting set of Madagascans consisted of bare-chested and bare-legged soldiers led by an officer turned out in a full-dress uniform, with red tunic, gold epaulets, and a fancy officer's hat topped by red and white feathers. Tuaregs, those fierce North African warriors who plagued

Accompanied by members of his general staff, Napoleon hurries toward the battlefield, which could be Austerlitz or Jena. As might be expected, Mignot produced many figures of the Napoleonic Wars.
Burtt Ehrlich Collection   Height: 75 mm

A platoon of Mignot French Napoleonic Marine Fusiliers of the Guard advances into battle.
Burtt Ehrlich Collection   Height: 55 mm

Mignot's version of the famed Polish Lancers that fought with
Napoleon.
Burtt Ehrlich Collection   Height: 75 mm

Waterloo-period Prussian hussars by Mignot advancing at the trot.
Burtt Ehrlich Collection   Height: 75 mm

If Napoleon had conquered England, he might have arrived at Buckingham Palace in a full-size model of this Mignot Napoleonic coach.
Burtt Ehrlich Collection

the Foreign Legion in romantic novels such as *Beau Geste*, as well as in real life, were produced, along with Chinese Boxers, sets of Siamese infantry and Royal Guards, and Indian Army troops in turbans (catalogued as "Hindous").

The period leading up to and including World War I (1890–1920) saw an explosion of sets depicting French and foreign military units. Topical sets included Russian and Japanese troops from the 1904–5 war; while the troubled Balkans were represented by Bulgarians, Serbians, and Rumanians. Then, too, there were Turkish, Greek, and Spanish troops. The major nations that participated in the Great War were added to the lineup: English, Belgian, Austrian, and Russian troops in khaki or their active-service equivalents. Prussians appeared in their field-gray uniforms and spiked helmets, later changed to coal-scuttle helmets; German cavalry included dragoons, hussars, and cuirassiers in full dress, and Uhlans (lancers) in dress and field gray; the English mounted arm featured Life Guards, hussars, and dragoons, and troopers in khaki service dress with peaked caps. There were Italian and Belgian Lancers, and a particularly fine set of the Russian Imperial Guard in their crested eagle helmets. When the Yanks arrived "over there" to pay their debt to Lafayette, Mignot paid tribute to the Americans by issuing infantry and cavalry in khaki uniforms, with the familiar campaign hats still favored by Marine Corps drill instructors and National Park Service Rangers. (American infantry could also be had in steel helmets.)

All of these troops and their French counterparts came in a few basic positions: *au pas* (marching), *au feu* (standing firing), *à genoux au feu* (kneeling firing), *couchée au feu* (lying firing), and *à l'assaut* (charging). (Two other infantry positions, *fixe* (attention) and *au repos* (at ease) were used almost exclusively for troops of earlier periods.) Cavalry were either on standing, trotting, or galloping horses, the trotting horse, with its queer forward lean, being the most common; only after World War I was a charging horse added to the range. Indeed, economy of position marked virtually all of Mignot's figures, and the firm's lack of imagination in posturing stands in marked contrast to the spirited animation of Heyde's toy soldiers and those of other German makers.

But there was certainly variety enough in the vast array of French troops turned out by the company in the thirty-year span from 1890 to the Treaty of Versailles. More than 60 types of infantry and 15 types of mounted troops of the regular French Army (not counting French colonial troops) were issued in the standard boxed sets of 12 infantry or 6 cavalry figures. This is a rather impressive number of sets, considering that Mignot managed to cover Napoleon's Grande Armée with fewer than 20 sets of infantry and 11 of cavalry and mounted artillerymen.

Many of the pre-1914 and World War I French Army sets were merely variations on a theme. For example, French Infantry of the Line in greatcoats (*capote*) could be had in all of the basic positions—marching, attacking, and in the three firing positions, as well as marching at double time (*pas gymnastique*) and marching with slung arms (*fusil bretelle*). Before 1914, the line infantry were dressed in natty blue tunics or greatcoats and red trousers and képis (forage caps). With the outbreak of the war, Mignot put them into horizon-blue active-service uniforms with shrapnel-proof helmets. Among the other infantry units of this period were Chasseurs à Pied, Marine Infantry and Marine Fusiliers, Gendarmes (military police), Gardes de Paris, military cadets from Saint Cyr, and the famed mountain troops, the Alpine Chasseurs. The St. Cyrien cadets were shown marching in their full-dress uniforms with plumed shakos, which, incredibly, they wore when they charged against German machine guns during the 1914 fighting in the Ardennes.

Mignot got especially good mileage out of its Alpine Chasseur model. Besides a standard marching set in berets and dress-blue uniforms, the Chasseurs also appeared on skis and as gunners in a Mountain Artillery set that included a mule-drawn howitzer and another gun broken down in sections and carried on the backs of pack mules. Finally, there was a special three-tier display set that celebrated the heroic actions of the Alpine troops

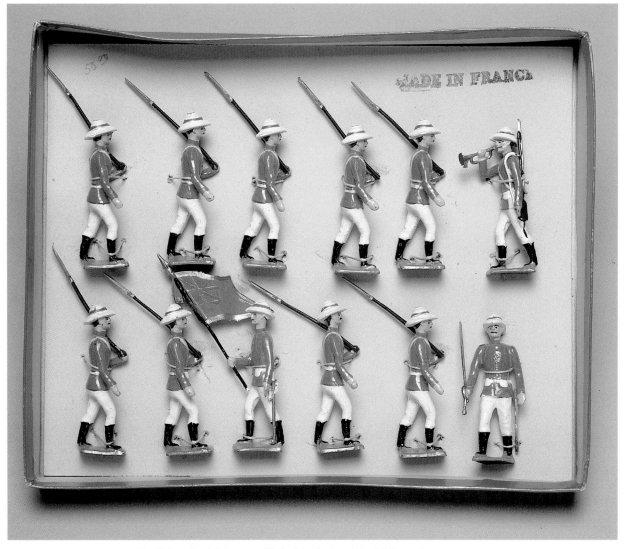

English colonial troops still tied in their original Mignot box.
Burtt Ehrlich Collection   Height: 55 mm

French tourists (right) check out the local color in this Mignot
display set of a North African village scene.
Burtt Ehrlich Collection

North African Tuaregs attack a unit of
French colonial infantry backed up by
mounted Spahis in this grouping by Mignot.
Burtt Ehrlich Collection

Height: Foot figures: 55 mm
Mounted: 75 mm

North African Goumiers, like these by
Mignot, served as scouts for the French
Army in North Africa.
Burtt Ehrlich Collection   Height: 75 mm

during the campaign in the Vosges Mountains. White-clad Chasseurs and a Mountain Artillery gun team were shown marching against a scenic backdrop of snow-covered mountains. Included were trees, a wooden cabin, and a bridge, and the set could be obtained in five sizes with as few as 29 or as many as 89 pieces.

The changing weaponry of modern warfare was taken into account. While there was still plenty of horse-drawn transport—gun teams, ambulances, field forges, and kitchens—tanks and other mechanized military vehicles were added to the line. The French "75," considered the best fieldpiece of its day, replaced older-model cannons in the various artillery sets. Special boxes designated "Battery" and "Heavy Artillery" featured simulated brick-and-concrete bunkers and fortifications, as well as large cannons of various types, in fixed emplacements or hauled by motorized lorries. Grenade-throwing infantrymen joined their rifle-toting comrades, and there were machine-gun sections (called *mitrailleurs*), motorcycle companies, and a modern communications display, "*Télégraphie Militaire*," with telegraph poles, telegraphers seated at tables, and horse-drawn vehicles.

A British toy soldier enthusiast recalls an imposing display set entitled "1914–1918 War," available in four sizes ranging from 41 to 127 pieces, which "contained trenches attacked by German infantry and manned by French grenade throwers, no-man's-land with ruined buildings and close fighting, dugouts and heavy gun positions with an observer on a ladder." Another World War I set, "Chars d'Assaut," included tanks in camouflage colors, with revolving turrets and moving treads, leading infantry into action.

Every war has its casualties and Mignot saw to the comfort of the wounded in its "Medical Service" sets, which came complete with stretcher teams, various figures of wounded soldiers, a motorized ambulance, and even a hospital complete with beds and adequately staffed by doctors, medical orderlies, and demure, wasp-waisted nurses in long skirts. The mundane side of soldiering was represented by work parties, or *hommes de corvée*, as the French called them, dressed in white fatigue smocks and either helmets or soft caps. And busily engaged they were: some pushed wheelbarrows or carried piles of straw or sacks on their shoulders, while others policed the grounds with brooms or trooped off to their work details shouldering picks, shovels, and hammers.

When not marching off to the wars or building bridges and fortifications, the toy troops could retire to scale-model barracks made of wood. Barracks for infantry (*caserne d'infanterie*) and for cavalry (*quartier de cavalerie*) came in several sizes and featured removable fronts. The interior had beds, rifle racks, and assorted paraphernalia; in the case of the two-story cavalry barracks, the upstairs contained living quarters for the troops, while the lower level provided stables for their mounts.

Like Heyde, Mignot turned back the pages of history and produced a notable line of troops representing the armies of the past. The firm's *soldats des temps anciens* (soldiers of former times) were among its finest offerings, and Mignot's justifiable pride in the accuracy of details of uniforms and equipment was evident in the catalogue statement that "All of these soldiers are created on the basis of documents found in various museums, notably the Museum of the Army, as well as from books and models."

A look at the ancient troops in the series bears out this attention to historical detail. Mignot originally produced four types of ancient infantry: Romans, Greeks, Egyptians, and Gauls (Assyrians were added later). The Roman infantry were superb recreations of the legionaries who followed Caesar and his successors on their campaigns of conquest. Mignot's Romans wore the close-fitting, visor-less helmet called the *cassis*, or the more ornate Attic-style helmet, along with an accurate rendition of the *lorica segmentata*, a linen jacket on which was sewn strips of brass armor, and tight-fitting trousers called *braccae*. Ordinary legionaries carried either a *pilum*, the short thrusting or throwing spear, or a *gladius Ibericus*, the efficient, double-edged Roman broadsword; and all were further equipped with the curved, oblong legionary

A group of ferocious Dahomean warriors, including a chief holding a severed head.
Burtt Ehrlich Collection   Height: 55 mm

One of the more colorful Mignot bands was this marching musical corps of the famed French Zouaves.
Burtt Ehrlich Collection   Height: 55 mm

A prewar Mignot box lid
with a multicolored label
showing medals won
at various toy expositions.
Burtt Ehrlich Collection

Before World War II,
Mignot boxes sometimes
carried a list of available
sets on the inside of the lid.
Burtt Ehrlich Collection

A rare group of African warriors by Mignot.
Burtt Ehrlich Collection   Height: 55 mm

71

shield. Each 12-piece set came with an *aquilifer* (standard-bearer) holding the eagle-topped legion standard, and a centurion holding a *fasces*, or ceremonial ax in the center of a bundle of rods.

Egyptians came in more colorful garb and with a variety of weapons, including bows, swords, and spears, and elaborate standards; Greeks were shown in their Corinthian helmets with horsehair crests, holding their lavishly decorated round shields in one hand and a sword or spear in the other. The Gauls, in their furskin cloaks and winged helmets, were a particularly fierce lot, hacking away at their adversaries with swords and double-headed axes. L. W. Richards, whose extensive research on Mignot appeared in the British Model Soldier Society *Bulletin*, offered this wry description of a special three-tier display box of Gauls and Romans: "The Gauls defended a palisaded village which had round huts, dogs, open fires, an idol and a priestess with raised arm rousing the troops. The exhortations seemed very necessary as there were plenty of Roman soldiers."

Historical sets also included Franks, Crusaders and their Saracen foes, mounted and foot knights, and archers marching and in action from the period of Joan of Arc. It was natural that the legendary Maid of Orléans should have inspired Mignot to produce special display sets. An interesting two-tier scenic display box shows Joan, standard held aloft, leading her soldiers against an English fortress on one level, while on the second tier she is mounted at the head of a victory procession entering a captured town.

Continuing through the centuries, Mignot produced a set of gaily costumed 15th-century halberdiers in relaxed pose, one hand resting on the hip, the other holding a halberd. There were infantry from the periods of Francis I and Henry IV, and for youngsters who wanted to re-create the exploits of D'Artagnan and his comrades Athos, Porthos, and Aramis, colorful sets of Louis XIII's musketeers in their wide-brimmed feathered hats. The musketeers came both mounted and on foot, and there were sets of Cardinal Richelieu's guards to complement them. The French Army of the late 17th and early 18th centuries was represented by infantry of Louis XIV in white, blue, and red uniforms—half the troops armed with muskets and the rest with pikes—and by three regiments of the Garde Française in white, black, and red uniforms.

Historical cavalry sets included mounted Gauls, Crusaders, and knights, as well as French cavalry regiments from the time of Henry IV to that of Louis XVI. Except for the knights, who could be had on either trotting or galloping horses, all of the historical cavalry were at the trot. After World War II, Mignot expanded its line of mounted historical figures to include Roman and Greek cavalry, Huns (properly barbarous in appearance), and Franks. Surely the *pièce de résistance* of the firm's postwar originals was a ferocious group of French Revolutionaries during the Reign of Terror. The set consisted of peasant men and women marching off to the barricades armed with pikes, scythes, pitchforks, and rakes. Two of them carry poles upon which are impaled the blood-drenched heads of a male and a female aristocrat—an uncharacteristically gruesome touch for Mignot.

Especially fine was Mignot's series "Historical Personages." Many of history's most famous names were included, the ancients being represented by Ramses II, Cleopatra, Nebuchadnezzar, Julius Caesar, and the Gallic chief Vercingetorix. Among others in Mignot's "Who's Who" of history were Attila, Richard the Lion-Heart and his foe Saladin, Cardinal Richelieu, Mary Queen of Scots, England's Charles I, and Pope Pius VII. The New World was not forgotten, and the span of American history from 1492 to 1865 was neatly summed up by figures of Christopher Columbus, George Washington, and Abraham Lincoln. Naturally, there was an abundance of French kings, queens, and emperors from Charlemagne to Napoleon III. Mignot added to the list well into the 1950s until there were nearly 100 personalities. About half of these were equestrian figures, most often on a rearing horse, which when mounted on a wooden base—as were all of the personality figures after World War II—conveyed the impression of a typical park statue.

At the time of the Boer War, Mignot brought out models of the sturdy Dutch farmers who fought the British Army to a standstill.
Burtt Ehrlich Collection   Height: 75 mm

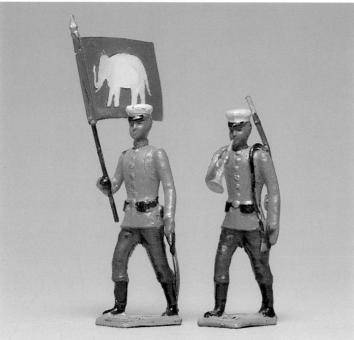

Siamese Royal Guardsmen, one of two Siamese military units produced by Mignot.

British colonial troops, including turbaned Sikhs from India, are on parade in this special mammoth display set by Mignot.

Burtt Ehrlich Collection

Height: Foot figures: 55 mm
Mounted: 75 mm

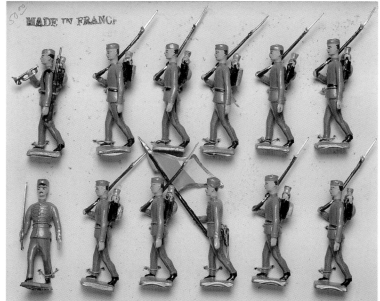

World War I received extensive coverage from Mignot and included the troops of minor nations such as Serbia, Rumania, and Bulgaria. A marching unit of Serbian infantry is seen in the boxed set.
Burtt Ehrlich Collection   Height: 55 mm

A group of Mignot British cavalrymen of World War I.
Burtt Ehrlich Collection   Height: 75 mm

The postwar years saw the introduction of a series of French standard-bearers carrying the regimental flags and royal standards of France from the 16th century to the Napoleonic Wars. Each of the finely crafted figures is individually mounted on a wooden base, with a printed paper label proclaiming the name of the regiment and the date (for example, "Royal Roussillon, 1680"). The flags are almost fully unfurled so that every detail, including the mottoes in French or Latin, are visible. The quality of the painting and the exquisite detail raise these figures above the level of toy soldiers to that of display pieces, and in fact they are so regarded by collectors fortunate enough to have acquired any of them.

Alone among the major toy soldier manufacturers, Mignot produced troops of the Israeli Army shortly after the creation of the Jewish state in 1948. The Israelis wore British-style helmets, shorts, and shirts with rolled-up sleeves; they came in action, with soldiers carrying rifles and machine guns, and throwing grenades, and included an officer and the inevitable standard-bearer—a trademark of virtually all of Mignot's military sets.

Ever-mindful of a growing American market, the French firm issued a series of American Civil War soldiers, both Union and Confederate, in the 1950s. Infantry came in all of the basic positions—marching, assaulting, and firing in different positions—while the cavalry were mounted on charging horses, the troopers holding sabers fully extended in front of them. Since the Union troops wore uniforms patterned after those of contemporary French line-infantry units, the Federals were more accurately represented than their Rebel foes. Union soldiers wore the familiar dark-blue képis, dark-blue tunics, and sky-blue trousers; and infantry officers were clothed in full-dress frock coats with fringed gold epaulets and Hardee hats with plumes. A curious version of Confederate infantry in the possession of the author shows them in porkpie hats and skin-tight trousers, making them look a bit like Puritans in leotards. Certainly these Southern troops bear little resemblance to the real Johnny Rebs they are supposed to represent.

The Civil War series included horse-drawn field artillery units and gunners, along with ambulances complete with stretcher-bearers and casualties. There were Union and Confederate labor battalions and figures of the principal commanders, generals U. S. Grant and Robert E. Lee, both, interestingly, mounted on Lucotte horses. The Lee figure is particularly striking, showing the gray-haired Confederate leader holding his hat aloft, as if acknowledging the cheers of his troops. Mignot also produced West Point cadets marching in winter and summer uniforms, and an extremely well-done West Point color guard, with the national standard and the U. S. Military Academy flag.

In addition to their first-grade 55-millimeter figures, Mignot issued an extensive line of semiround toy soldiers (*soldats fins ½ massifs*) in 32- and 40-millimeter scale with cavalrymen proportionally larger. The focus here was on the French Army from the Revolution to World War I, with a sampling of the foreign troops and native warriors of the 1890–1914 period found in the 55-millimeter range. Following the pattern of the German semisolids, the horses of the cavalrymen were not quite three-dimensional, while the detachable riders were more full bodied. At least one authority found Mignot's small-scale figures of the Middle Ages "not so effective . . . as those of later periods," and noted with some disdain that they "are curiously reminiscent of archaic French cathedral sculpture."

On the other hand, the small-scale range included several interesting display sets, among them an encampment of French troops (c. 1910), with conical tents, sentry box, trees, shrubs, camp equipage, a staff car, and soldiers variously occupied. There were large sets depicting the colonial wars in Morocco and also naval warfare, the latter consisting of small-scale semiround ships. A series of 45 metal models traced the history of the warship from the days of the Viking longships to World War II. There were Spanish galleons, the famed trio of vessels that Columbus commanded on his voyage to the New World, a 17th-century man-of-war, models of the *Monitor* and the *Merrimac*, a slew of modern French war-

With the coming of World War I, Mignot added motorized transport
to its miniature army. Here we see an ambulance and a lorry, both
made of tinplate, accompanied by French line infantry in shrapnel-
proof helmets.

Burtt Ehrlich Collection   Height: 55 mm

Mignot marine infantry, still stitched into its original box. Note the paper labels underneath the bases with the words "Made in France."
Burtt Ehrlich Collection

Height: 55 mm

Celebrating the exploits of the famed Alpine Chasseurs in World War I, Mignot issued a special multitiered display set showing the Chasseurs and a Mountain Artillery unit on campaign in the Vosges Mountains—complete with a cabin and various scenic props.
Burtt Ehrlich Collection

Cannons are unlimbered as a battery of French Mountain Artillery
by Mignot goes into action.
Burtt Ehrlich Collection   Height: 55 mm

Alpine Chasseur ski troops glide across a snowy landscape.
Burtt Ehrlich Collection   Height: 55 mm

ships, and several American battleships and carriers, including the *Missouri* and the *Saratoga*. Civilian vesels included early paddle wheelers, a 19th-century American show boat, cargo ships, and, to create a proper harbor, a jetty with lighthouse and a pier with cranes and storage tanks.

The success of British-made hollow-cast figures resulted in the creation by Mignot of similar figures, called *soldats ordinaires creux*. Reporting on this line, which of course included an abundance of French Napoleonic and World War I troops, L. W. Richards wrote in the British Model Soldier Society *Bulletin*:

Second grade Mignot figures were many and varied, and they were hollowcast and produced between the wars.... In general they were sub-standard in comparison with the first grade but nevertheless contained many interesting types, some quite out of the ordinary run of model soldiers.... The size ranged from 52 to 80 millimeters.

Romans, Knights and Archers were in good supply and some of the Knights on horseback had movable arms. Warriors of Africa and Arabs plentifully robed were a large series. There was one in particular dancing with two scimitars crossed above his head. Figures of Zulus larger than standard size look really terrifying. Turkish and other cavalry wearing the fez were of all sizes. Some looked grotesque. A few had movable arms. A whole set of Matelots [French sailors] were quite out of the ordinary. There was a Naval Officer at the wheel of a ship and others looking through telescopes and binoculars. Matelots, some in blue but mostly in white, were kneeling with scrubbing brush and pail, sitting and holding a saucepan, carrying kitbags, throwing the contents of a bucket, [carrying] an anchor, pulling a line, and blowing a bugle.

Finally Mignot produced a line of lightweight, unbreakable toy soldiers made of aluminum. They were generally rather simple in design and paintwork, but because they were cheap and durable, found a wide market. The unbreakable figures were large size (60 mm or more) and came in only a few basic marching and action positions.

Civilian themes were not neglected by Mignot; and the firm, aware of the fact that nearly every young boy yearns to be a fire fighter and that all children love the circus, issued impressive display sets of French Pompiers (fire fighters) and circus scenes. The Pompiers were a dashing lot in their dark-blue uniforms and brass-colored helmets. They were shown in action, carrying axes, ladders, buckets, and other pieces of fire equipment; and sets came with an officer carrying orders, a trumpeter, and—with a characteristic Gallic touch—a fire fighter carrying a woman dressed in a flimsy nightgown who presumably had just been rescued from a blazing building. Larger display boxes had horse-drawn—later motorized—fire engines, and smaller hose carts and pumpers, each pulled rickshaw-style by two Pompiers. A wooden "Caserne de Pompiers" (fire station) with removable front was also available.

Circus display sets reproduced quite realistically the interior of a "big top." Clowns, acrobats, lion tamers, and many other familiar circus performers were to be had in large diorama boxes with a backdrop of an audience watching from the two levels of a grandstand. Children, of course, are fascinated by animals, and Mignot accommodated this interest in a series of sets re-creating a *jardin d'acclimation*, or zoo, which included illuminated metal diorama boxes.

Agricultural activities were encouraged by a range of farm displays (also available in semiround 40-mm scale), including a model farm with an impressive two-story farmhouse, an assortment of animals, trees, picket and rail fences, and an ordinary working farm, with a simple cottage, plenty of chickens, pigs, sheep, goats, and cows, horse-drawn carts, and the usual trees, shrubs, and fences. The ordinary farm could be had in seven sizes (the semiround in nine), with as few as 21 or as many as

Marine fusiliers debark from a rare Mignot tin boat.
Burtt Ehrlich Collection   Height: 55 mm

Mignot soldiers not only fought and marched, they
also worked at policing the grounds.
Burtt Ehrlich Collection   Height: 55 mm

Serving the needs of troops in the field, this cantinière and her wagonload of provisions follow in the wake of the army.
Burtt Ehrlich Collection   Height: 55 mm

A horde of Gauls sweeps down on the disciplined ranks of one of Julius Caesar's Roman Legions.
Burtt Ehrlich Collection   Height: 55 mm

Mignot took great pride in the accuracy of its historical figures. The firm's range of ancient troops included these fierce-looking Gauls (left) and sturdy Roman infantry.
Burtt Ehrlich Collection   Height: 55 mm

The legendary exploits of Joan of Arc received special attention from Mignot. In the two-tier diorama above, we see the Maid of Orléans leading her troops in battle on the lower level, then heading a triumphant procession through a captured city on the upper level.
Burtt Ehrlich Collection   Height: 55 mm

179 pieces, while the model farm came in five sizes of 40 to 135 pieces.

There were elaborate hunt scenes, too, with shotgun-toting hunters and huntresses, gun-bearers and beaters, and lots of rabbits and assorted fowl to be picked off; desert caravans with camels and camelmen, Arab potentates and their guards, and enough palm trees to create a small oasis; and at the other end of the climate spectrum, sets representing Admiral Byrd's expedition to the South Pole, complete with a backdrop of glacial formations that realistically represented the Antarctic wastelands.

Religious themes were also covered. Au Plat d'Etain catalogues of the 1930s illustrate a Roman Catholic procession, with robed clerical figures, nuns, and other participants carrying banners. In the 1930s, Mignot issued a set depicting High Mass, which included the celebrant, deacon and subdeacon, choir, and congregation. From time to time, the company issued novelty items, among them a charming pair of semiflat figures of the comic film stars Laurel and Hardy.

Mignot's method of production has remained fairly constant in the century and a half since the firm of C. B. G. began producing toy soldiers. The first-grade 55-millimeter solid figures are made of a lead alloy, with weapons and accoutrements, such as rifles, packs, bayonets, sword scabbards, and flags, separately cast and soldered onto the figures. Heads, too, are separately cast and, in the manner of Germanic solids, are plugged into the bodies, resulting at times in a slightly elongated neck. Infantry figures appear on squarish bases usually painted khaki or a grayish brown. Pre–World War II Mignot figures had no engraved markings under the base, although sometimes a blue-and-white paper label with the words "Made in France" was affixed to the underside. After the war, the designation "C. B. G." or "C. B. G. Made in France" was generally engraved on the underside of the bases. Until the 1960s, Mignot figures were painted in a semigloss finish. Subsequently, glossy enamels were used until the early 1980s, when a switch was made to a matte finish.

Casting and painting have always been by hand, and production techniques as well as working conditions have changed little over the past 150 years. This is confirmed by the occasional foreign visitor to the Mignot factory, which until 1981 was located in a centuries-old building near the Place de la République. (It is now situated in another part of Paris.) Following such a visit in the 1940s, an American collector reported:

After entering a dark doorway and climbing a narrow staircase upon which I expected to meet Charlotte Corday or Madame LeFarge, I arrived in the musty twilight of the factory. First I was ushered into [Henri Mignot's] private office where there were several dioramas recently displayed at the Union Française exhibition, now unconcernedly perched on an old cabinet and threatening to crash to the floor. . . .

Finally we surveyed the production routines starting with the foundry deep in the bowels of the building, where by the light of a single unshaded bulb, two elderly men and a woman were casting. . . . A stroll through the finishing room where deftly working women trimmed the pieces as they arrived from the foundry was followed by a look at the assembling room. Here Roman Legionnaires by the century were being issued shields. Last came the painting [room], where half a dozen women, each at her own bench working at a piece rate, rapidly painted figures arranged, several score of the same type, on trays.

Some thirty years later, Professor George Keester found that—except for the death of Henry Mignot and a reduction in the size of the staff—the general operation had remained much the same. Recalling his 1978 visit to the factory, Professor Keester gave this account of the experience:

I had been told by collector friends that tracking down the Mignot factory would be something of an adventure, which it was. The ostensible address was 32 rue

Ancient Egyptian troops by Mignot march across the desert against a backdrop of the Pyramids.
Burtt Ehrlich Collection

Height: 55 mm

A medieval French herald trumpeter by Mignot sounds a call, perhaps summoning gallant knights to a joust.
Henry Kurtz Collection   Height: 55 mm

For those children who wanted to re-create the exploits of D'Artagnan and the Three Musketeers, made famous by Alexandre Dumas, Mignot produced these French musketeers of Louis XIII.
Henry Kurtz Collection   Height: Foot figures: 55 mm
Mounted: 75 mm

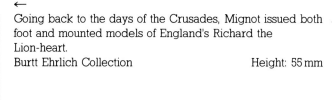

← Going back to the days of the Crusades, Mignot issued both foot and mounted models of England's Richard the Lion-heart.
Burtt Ehrlich Collection   Height: 55 mm

In this detail shot, we see a colorfully uniformed figure of a Mignot infantryman of Francis I.
Henry Kurtz Collection   Height: 55 mm

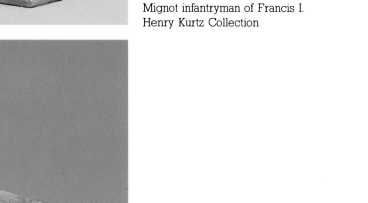

Mignot produced an extensive range of historical personality figures. Emphasis was on the kings of France, such as this equestrian model of Francis I, and French military leaders.
Burtt Ehrlich Collection   Height: 75 mm

Infantry and cavalry of Henry IV of France were among the
historical types issued by Mignot.
Burtt Ehrlich Collection   Height: Foot figures: 55 mm
                                              Mounted: 75 mm

Charlot, a narrow side street near the historic Place de la République. Actually, as we discovered after poking around, the building was really in an alley off the rue Charlot. Here we came upon a three-sided building enclosing a large courtyard. We walked through the wooden gates into the courtyard and spotted a small, battered sign stating "Mignot (CBG)" over a dingy doorway.

The winding stairway beyond the door led to the second floor reception area. We were greeted in a friendly but reserved manner and were informed that although two members of the Mignot family were still alive, they were no longer actively involved in the operation of the business. The room we were first shown was a rather dimly-lit showroom, which was probably the original office of Henri Mignot. Now it had been converted, by means of rough shelving, into a tiny museum of sorts, where many of the old figures and sets are displayed. Not far from this room, on the same floor, a young woman stood behind a counter wrapping parcels of sets. Apparently, this was the shipping department.

We then went down a dark, twisting backstairs to the casting department. On the way into another first floor room, we passed piles of metal ingots and were allowed to glimpse shelves full of hinged, brass box moulds, many covered with dust and looking as though they had not been used since World War I. There were several large melting pots set in brick pits, with metal exhausts overhead, and a casting table next to each. Only one of these was being used. A young man, bare to the waist, and working under the light of a single 40-watt bulb, was hand-casting some 30 mm flats. It was very warm in the room and, as far as I could see, there was little ventilation. In the same room, at tables located near the windows, sat another young man and an older woman. They were hand-soldering various parts to a pile of figures they plucked from boxes next to their tables.

Next we were led through a back courtyard to another room of similar size. Here we found only one person, a woman, painting figures at a table near a window. We were told that there was a third floor where additional painters worked and where figures were sewn into cardboard boxes, but since no one was working there at the time, the tour came to an end and we were shown out the back door with assurances we would be welcome again.

The factory setup and methods of manufacture were straight out of the early days of the Industrial Revolution and go a long way to explain the scarcity of Mignot figures.

The manner in which Mignot's toy troops were packaged remained fairly constant as well over the decades. Boxes were made of heavy cardboard, with a red paper covering and yellow or gold trim around the edges of the lid. Labels affixed to the center of the lid show slight variations, the earliest bearing the words "Fabrique Française" and "Paris" in large type, with "C. B. G."—the manufacturer's mark—sandwiched in between, and with reproductions of medals won in 1878 and 1900 prominently displayed. Between the world wars, a dressier four-color label was used which, in addition to the manufacturer's statements and medals, had illustrations of a French cuirassier and a line infantryman in uniforms of the 1890–1914 period. More recently, Mignot adopted a yellow label with the words *Les Soldats de Plomb* in bold lettering and line drawings of a Zulu warrior on one side and French soldiers, including an Alpine Chasseur, on the other.

The basic 55-millimeter Mignot sets, as earlier noted, comprised either 12 infantry or 6 cavalrymen, the troops being sewn in two rows to a light-colored backing card that could be inserted into the box. The standard infantry and cavalry sets nearly always came with an officer, a standard-bearer, and a drummer or a bugler for infantry or a trumpeter for cavalry. Before World War II, basic sets with larger numbers of figures—from 18 to 60 infantry or 9 to 24 cavalry—were available. Special display sets might

An ornately garbed figure of Louis XIV.
Burtt Ehrlich Collection   Height: 55 mm

Mignot also provided an equestrian version of Louis XIV mounted on
a rearing horse.
Henry Kurtz Collection   Height: 55 mm

In this unusual set by Mignot, French peasants armed with scythes, rakes, pitchforks, and other makeshift weapons look very much as they probably did on the day they stormed the Bastille.
Henry Kurtz Collection   Height: 55 mm

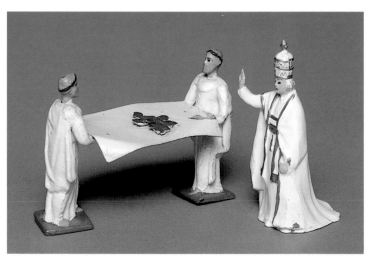

Among the major toy soldier makers, Mignot was the only one to produce soldiers of the Israeli Army, issued in a mixture of civilian garb and British-style uniforms.
Burtt Ehrlich Collection   Height: 55 mm

Among the major toy soldier makers, Mignot was the only one to produce soldiers of the Israeli Army, issued in a mixture of civilian garb and British-style uniforms. Palm trees by Britains.
Burtt Ehrlich Collection   Height: 55 mm

contain up to 200 pieces or more.

When production resumed after World War II, Mignot issued only infantry boxes of 12 and cavalry boxes with 6 figures. (Later the cavalry sets were reduced to 5 figures.) In the 1960s, the firm also put out 8-piece infantry boxes and 4-piece "mini-sets" in cellophane-fronted display boxes with the C. B. G. crest. Individual cavalry figures and both foot and mounted personality figures were also issued this way.

Production methods and packaging may have remained fairly constant during the past century, but prices have changed dramatically. In the years before World War II, a standard set of 12 infantry cost 27 francs, just over $1, while band sets were priced slightly higher at 30 francs. Cavalry sets were naturally more expensive, the standard set of six mounted troops costing 46 francs, about $1.40. Individual infantry figures were available for as little as 3.50 francs (10 cents) for an ordinary foot soldier and about 25 cents for a cavalryman.

Prices shot up rapidly after the war (in the United States in the early 1950s, Mignot figures averaged $8 to $9 for a basic set). Nevertheless, even as late as 1970 a set of Mignot figures could be purchased in many American stores for $15. Today, with factory production sharply curtailed, new-issue Mignot sets average about $150 in those few retail outlets that still stock them, while older (pre–World War II) and rarer sets have sold for $300 to $400 and more at auction.

Dominant as it long has been in France, Mignot did face some local competition. In the early 1900s, Cherband of Paris produced fully round lead soldiers of no special distinction. Later, in the 1930s, Maurice Berne issued a more extensive range of standard-size toy soldiers (55–60 mm) of different periods in lead, aluminum, and composition. John G. Garratt, citing a 1935 catalogue, notes that the Berne line featured "modern and Napoleonic French troops of all kinds (including portrait models of Napoleon and Joffre), German, Scottish, Russian, American and Italian combatants, and the inevitable Cowboys and Indians." Civilian types were also produced, among them

circus, zoo, railway, and hunting figures. Berne also manufactured aluminum cannons, vehicles, ships, and planes under the Rivollet trademark.

Aluminum figures were manufactured by several other French companies. Beginning in the 1930s, Quiralu issued a reasonably well designed line of predominantly French troops, packaged in sets of seven or more and boxed in simple, thin-cardboard cartons, with the words *"Quiralu–Jouets Français—Incassable"* (French toys—unbreakable) in orange-red lettering on one side. The figures were fixed-arm, approximately 65 millimeters, and sets normally included an officer and a standard-bearer with removable flag. Quiralu appears to have shared its molds with Frenchal, another aluminum toy soldier maker, and may also have furnished designs to Wend-Al in England. The company ceased to exist as an independent entity around 1960.

Following World War II, Commandant Henri Borie of Saint Aignon-Orléans put out some excellent 30-millimeter semisolid figures, focusing on the French Revolution and Napoleonic periods. Boxed under the heading *"Figur: Le Soldat de Plomb Historique,"* the models included British and American soldiers of the American Revolutionary War, British and French colonial troops, and a sampling of soldiers and warriors of more exotic lands such as Turkey, Arabia, and China. Sets contained 5 to 20 foot figures, or 5 to 12 cavalry. Although toy-soldier-like in their charm and general appearance, the superior design and painting lift them a large notch above the typical playroom figures. Figur miniatures were produced from about 1950 to 1965.

During the 1940s, a French military artist named Auger created and painted a series of French Army standard-bearers. Bearing a strong similarity to the figures of Mignot—to the point where they are often mistaken for the latter—but somewhat larger (65 mm) and even finer in quality, they were available for a relatively short time. Like the Figur miniatures, they were really military miniatures made in toy soldier style. Marcel Baldet, in his book *Figurines et Soldats de Plomb*, cites

Early in its history Mignot provided toy soldiers for the American market, such as these rare U.S. infantrymen in 1890s uniforms.
Burtt Ehrlich Collection   Height: 55 mm

After World War II, Mignot exported to the United States a complete range of troops of the American Civil War. Here we see Union and Confederate cavalry in a head-on clash of the sort that took place at Brandy Station and Gettysburg.
Burtt Ehrlich Collection   Height: 75 mm

The Union High Command
was represented by General
Ulysses S. Grant. Both the
Lee and Grant figures were
mounted on Lucotte horses
and came with detachable
saddle trappings.
Henry Kurtz Collection
Height: 75 mm

Supposedly a Confederate
soldier, this curious-looking
fellow in a porkpie hat and
snug trousers is one of
Mignot's less successful
efforts.
Henry Kurtz Collection
Height: 55 mm

Included in Mignot's American range were West Point cadets in
both winter uniforms and summer dress.
Burtt Ehrlich Collection   Height: 55 mm

Mignot's personality figures of the American Civil War
featured this striking model of General Robert E. Lee
mounted on his horse, Traveler.
Henry Kurtz Collection   Height: 75 mm

Mignot did not neglect the prehistoric past, producing such unusual creatures as this dinosaur, which came individually boxed with an appropriate scenic backdrop.
Burtt Ehrlich Collection

Occasionally Mignot issued illuminated boxed dioramas such as this scene of jungle animals.
Burtt Ehrlich Collection

Auger's "series of standard-bearers of the Louis XVI to Revolution days, whose realistic banners seem to flap in the wind"; they are known to have been sold at Corr's in Washington, D.C., and several New York retail shops in the early 1950s. (Corr's 1952 catalogue carries an illustration of one figure and lists ten flag-bearers as then being available at $10 each.) The figures were painted in glossy enamels and mounted on wooden bases with the name of the regiment hand-lettered on a gold-colored label.

Berne, Cherband, Quiralu, Figur, and the others have faded into history, overwhelmed by the great wave of plastic toy troops, mostly marked "Made in Hong Kong," that has flooded the market in the past two decades. Only C. B. G. Mignot, the last holdout among the major manufacturers of traditional lead soldiers, still produces figures as it has since it entered the field in the 19th century. It is now the world's oldest continuously functioning manufacturer of toy soldiers.

Mexican banditos by Mignot hold up a train in a scene reminiscent of an old Hollywood movie.
Burtt Ehrlich Collection
Height: Foot figures: 55 mm
Mounted: 75 mm

The Paris fire brigade (Pompiers) swings into action with horse-drawn and mechanized fire-fighting equipment, rescuing a stricken woman from a blazing building. The Pompiers were undoubtedly the most colorful of Mignot's nonmilitary models.
Burtt Ehrlich Collection   Height: Foot figures: 55 mm

One of the more impressive Mignot display sets depicted Admiral
Byrd's Antarctic expedition and came complete with an Eskimo igloo
and a variety of wildlife.
Burtt Ehrlich Collection

Although the dominant French manufacturer of toy soldiers, Mignot faced competition from other local makers. In the 1930s, the firm of Quiralu issued a line of unbreakable soldiers made of aluminum, which included this set of St. Cyrien cadets.
Henry Kurtz Collection   Height: 65 mm

A splendidly animated troop of semiround 30mm Scots Greys cavalrymen by Commandant Henri Borie, who began producing his Figur line of toy soldiers after World War II.
Henry Kurtz Collection   Height: 30 mm

In the 1940s, a French artist named Auger issued a magnificent line of standard-bearers of the French Army, which, because of their appearance, are often confused with the figures of Mignot. The soldier in this detail shot holds the banner of the Regiment All. de Fersen.
Henry Kurtz Collection   Height: 65 mm

CHAPTER III
THE BRITISH MAKERS
The Rise of the Britains Empire

In 1930, at the age of fifty-six, Sir Winston Churchill published an account of his youthful adventures as a soldier and war correspondent. In it, he recalled that his decision to embark on a military career, which, in turn, served as his springboard into politics, was "entirely due" to his collection of toy soldiers. "I had ultimately nearly fifteen hundred," he wrote of his miniature army in *My Early Life: A Roving Commission*. "They were all of one size, all British, and organized as an infantry division with a cavalry brigade."

One afternoon, Lord Randolph Churchill, Sir Winston's father, decided to conduct a formal inspection of his son's lead battalions. Nearly fifty years later, the details of that day remained fresh in Sir Winston's memory, and he vividly described the incident in his autobiography:

All the troops were arranged in the correct formation of attack. My father spent twenty minutes studying the scene—which was really impressive—with a keen eye and a captivating smile. At the end he asked me if I would like to go into the Army. I thought it would be splendid to command an army, so I said "Yes" at once; and immediately was taken at my word. For years I thought my father with his experience and flair had discerned in me the qualities of military genius. But I was told later that he had only come to the conclusion that I was not clever enough to go to the Bar. However that may be, the toy soldiers turned the current of my life. Henceforward all my education was directed to passing into Sandhurst, and afterwards to the technical details of the profession of arms.

For the general reader, this incident, recounted with characteristic Churchillian wit, is interesting for its insight into how the future statesman was casually thrust into a military career. Of special interest to the serious toy soldier enthusiast, however, is the fact that the little metal troops Churchill played with as a child, and which "turned the current" of his life, were not of British manufacture. They could not have been. At the time young Winston was growing up at Blenheim Palace, in the early 1880s, there was not one commercial maker of lead soldiers in the whole of the British Isles. The toy soldiers that formed young Winston's miniature army were almost certainly imported from Germany. Although no full description of them is to be found in any of the standard works on Churchill's life, they were probably Heydes or the figures of another German manufacturer.

German-made toy soldiers dominated the British market until the last decade of the 19th century, despite the fact that British imperial power was at its height and that its soldiers occupied outposts of empire all over the globe. Indeed, the regimental flags of the Queen's army were laced with battle honors won in such exotic locales as Kandahar, Afghanistan, and Chillianwallah, India. During those late-19th-century years, there were gallant cavalry charges at Kassassin and Ulundi, and stirring feats of valor at Tel-el-Kebir during the Egyptian War of 1882 and at Rorke's Drift during the Zulu War of 1879. Yet when British schoolboys wanted to reenact these heroic engagements, they had to make do with lead soldiers pulled out of boxes marked "Dresden, Germany" and "Paris, France."

← To commemorate Queen Victoria's Diamond Jubilee in 1897, Britains issued a special souvenir display set of the Life Guards—its first military set—showing that famed regiment both in the uniforms worn in 1837, when Queen Victoria came to the throne, and in those worn in the late 1890s. Burtt Ehrlich Collection   Height: 70 mm

Long before they entered the toy soldier business, William Britain
and his sons produced a popular line of what they called "Automatic
and Scientific Clockwork Models and Toys," which included a
mechanical horse race designed so that the winner could not be
predicted.
Burtt Ehrlich Collection

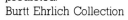

Don Quixote tilts at a windmill in this extremely rare Britains
mechanical toy dating from the turn of the century.
Burtt Ehrlich Collection   Height: Don Quixote: 60 mm
                                                      Windmill: 80 mm

An enterprising English toy maker named William Britain altered that situation in 1893, when he introduced a new line of attractively designed miniature soldiers that were less expensive than foreign imports. Up until then, the problems involved in producing metal soldiers competitive in quality and price with the figures of German and French firms had discouraged British manufacturers from challenging the Continental makers. But William Britain, as clever as he was ambitious, did not shrink from that challenge. For thirty years before he tried his hand at lead soldiers, Britain and several of his sons had been making intricate mechanical toys that were the delight of both children and adults. Britain's spring-operated money boxes—like the one consisting of a sailor who tossed a penny placed in his collection plate into an adjacent box, then tipped his hat and bowed—were extremely popular and often were used in the service of charitable causes.

A descriptive price list of Britain's "Automatic and Scientific Clockwork Models and Toys" dating from the 1880s offered such sure favorites as a mechanical bear that could run, move its head up and down and side to side, and even open its mouth "showing its teeth all the while in a most savage manner"; a mechanical footrace so contrived that the winner could not be predicted; and a scale model of a London road roller, which the catalogue somewhat haughtily stated was "made of solid castings, and not stamped tin like most of the foreign rubbish."

This same listing described a "machine gun" that—like a Gatling gun—used a crank handle to fire peas funneled through a cup on top of the gun barrel. With such a weapon, it was stated, a youngster could "put to rout brigade after brigade of toy soldiers, as fast as they can be formed." Roy Selwyn-Smith, formerly deputy chairman and technical director of Britains, speculates that the machine-gun peashooter may have inspired the Britains to get involved in the toy soldier trade. "It is quite possible," says Selwyn-Smith, "that William Britain may have purchased some solid lead soldiers to test the firepower of his machine gun. One of his sons, probably William, Jr., may have suggested that if the soldiers were hollow, like the

body and legs of 'The Walking Elephant,' another of Britain's novelties, they would be easier to knock over with the gun. Also, they could be cast much more quickly, without the delay of waiting for the lead to set, as in the case of solid castings."

Whatever the inspiration, Britain and his son, William, Jr., applied their creative talents and mechanical skills to the task of producing good but low-cost lead soldiers. In the early 1890s, after a series of experiments, William Britain, Jr.—generally acknowledged as the firm's inventive genius—successfully developed the first hollow-cast lead troops, and in so doing revolutionized the toy soldier industry. Unlike the solid figures of Heyde and Mignot, Britain's figures consisted only of a metal skin. Because the hollow-cast figures required much less metal than did the solids, they were cheaper to produce, less expensive to ship, and thus could be priced lower than German and French imports.

The process of creating the hollow-cast figures was an intricate one. Master models would first be carved out of wax, the sculptor in the early years being William, Jr., who served as the master modeler of the firm. The next stage was the creation of a two-piece metal mold that, when clamped together, formed a box with a spout where the metal, a lead alloy, could be poured in.

Casting was always done by hand—up to the final years of Britain-soldier production in the 1960s—and required dexterity and a keen sense of timing on the part of the craftsman. W. Y. Carman, a founder of the British Model Soldier Society, provides this description of the casting procedure in his book *Model Soldiers*: "The ingenious metal molds were made of two or more pieces of metal which hinged together to make a 'box' to hold the molten metal. A quick movement poured out the excess metal from the interior before all had chilled to the molds. The weight of the metal pressed the shell of the figure fully into the engraved details." As a further economy measure, the molds were designed so that the part where the head was cast could be removed and a variation substituted. In this way, a variety of regiments could be

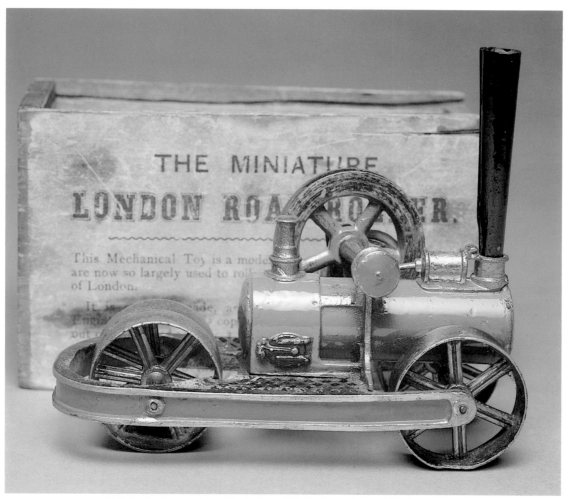

Britains took special pride in its solidly built scale model of a London road roller, which the firm's catalogue contrasted with poorly made imported tin toys.
Burtt Ehrlich Collection

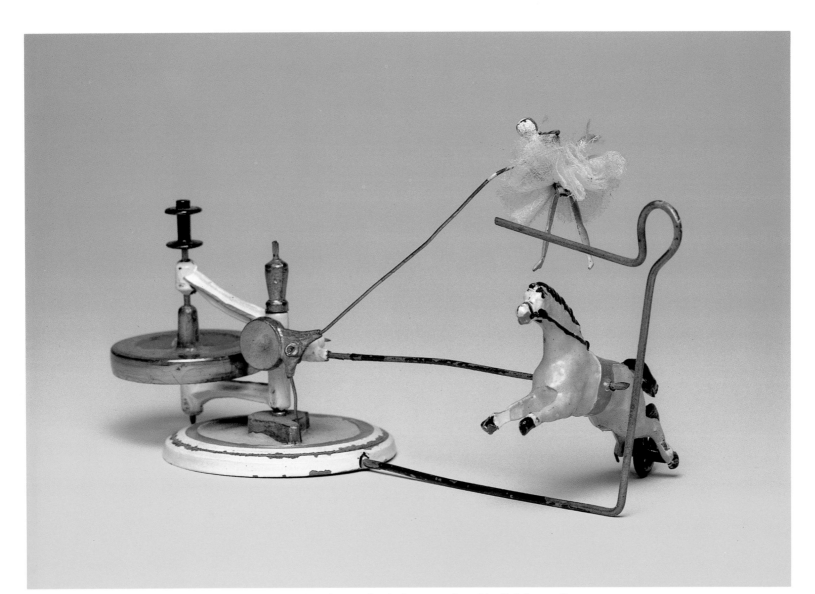

One of the charming mechanical toys produced by Britains; as the horse moves around in a circle, the lithe equestrienne jumps over the bar and lands on the horse's back.
Burtt Ehrlich Collection

106

A rare Britains waltzing couple, dating from the late
1890s.
Burtt Ehrlich Collection   Height: 85 mm

When the parasol above the rider was twirled, this Britains
mechanical elephant went for a walk.
Burtt Ehrlich Collection   Height; 140 mm

created by simply altering the head attached to a basic marching or running figure. This, incidentally, accounts for the characteristic thin neck in Britains models, since the neck size had to be kept slender in order to properly line up with the collar on the body.

From the beginning, William Britain & Sons (the firm's original designation) determined that their principal focus would be on toy troops representing the various regiments of the British Army and colonial troops from all parts of the empire. There would be no attempt to duplicate the extensive listings of Heyde or Mignot, whose miniature soldiers marched across the pages of history from antiquity to modern times. Britains lead-soldier production would remain firmly rooted in the British Army of that day, with occasional forays into history and the sporadic issuance of sets representing foreign armies then involved in a war—as, for example, the American and Spanish figures brought out in 1898 at the time of the Spanish–American War. Just how faithful Britains remained to its nationalistic emphasis is indicated in the composition of the first sets issued by the company between 1893 and 1901. Of the 125 numbered sets put on the market during that period, 104 were of British regiments, 15 represented colonial troops (primarily regiments of the Indian Army), and only six were of foreign military units.

The decision to concentrate on "British Soldiers" and "Soldiers of the British Empire"—as early box labels proudly proclaimed—was a sensible one. Not only was this a period of imperial glory and nationalistic fervor, but William Britain & Sons could see looming in the near future a great national celebration: Queen Victoria's Diamond Jubilee of 1897. What better time to bring out a line of British-made toy soldiers, they reasoned, and thus challenge German supremacy on playroom battlefields.

To further distinguish their figures from the Heydes and Heinrichs of Germany, Britains insisted on "strict attention being paid to accurate detail in colouring and uniform" of its British troops. No Britains-made Household Cavalryman would trot out of the soon-to-be-familiar oblong red boxes mounted on a *brown* horse—a blunder

committed by Heyde—for as William Britain, Jr., sneered, "Any British schoolboy knows better than that." (Britains Household Cavalry were, of course, properly mounted on black horses.) To ensure complete accuracy, the firm consulted appropriate regimental authorities, the War Office, and the College of Heralds.

All Britains figures were painted by hand, except for vehicles, which were usually dipped or, in later years, sprayed. Photographs of the company's North London factory, dating from the early 1900s, show young women in smocks hunched over long tables on which castings are lined up in neat rows. The girls were paid a piece rate on a per gross basis. "Each girl would have two or three gross of models standing before her on the bench," recalls a Britains official, "and she would completely paint the whole of this batch herself by going through the lot, painting one or two colors at a time and, in some cases, even three colors on one model before going on to the next. In fact, she might have had two brushes in her hand at one time if there were only small areas of different colours to be painted." If the figures in a particular set were all the same, then one or two girls would paint through the lot. But if a boxed set contained different types of models, the work would be divided among a group of girls, each one responsible for completely painting one type of model.

Britains had their first sets out on the market in 1893. With a polite and predictable bow to Buckingham Palace, the company chose for its premier offering the two regiments of Household Cavalry: The Life Guards (Set No. 1) and the Royal Horse Guards (Set No. 2). These were shortly joined by another cavalry unit, the 5th Dragoon Guards. All three sets used the same basic figures painted different colors. Compared to later efforts, the first figures were crude. The ponylike horse (later replaced by a sturdier cavalry mount) was a bit on the scrawny side, and the troopers had fixed arms with a strip of tin attached to simulate a sword. Later versions had movable arms with cast-lead swords.

During the first year of production, Britains also put out its first infantry set, the 7th Royal Fusiliers marching "at the

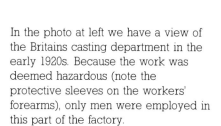

In the photo at left we have a view of the Britains casting department in the early 1920s. Because the work was deemed hazardous (note the protective sleeves on the workers' forearms), only men were employed in this part of the factory.

By far the largest part of the Britains work force was employed in the all-female painting department, seen below in this 1930s view of the more modern North Light Building to which the company had then recently relocated. The young women in the foreground are painting farm animals, which during that period were among Britains' most popular models.

Photos courtesy of Britains Ltd.

Forming up for inspection is this detachment of half-booted 7th Royal
Fusiliers, the first infantry set issued by Britains.
Burtt Ehrlich Collection   Height: 54 mm

Early figures of Scottish troops, like the Gordon and Black Watch Highlanders, had rifles plugged in at the cuff, which resulted in their being termed "plug-handed Highlanders."
Burtt Ehrlich Collection   Height: 54 mm

A later version of the Black Watch with a box designed by artist Fred Whisstock, whose illustrated labels were an important part of the packaging of Britains toy soldiers.
Burtt Ehrlich Collection   Height: 54 mm

slope" (the British equivalent of shoulder arms). The soldiers were outfitted in their distinctive black busbies, scarlet tunics, and blue trousers tucked into half boots. The rifle and hand holding it were cast separately and plugged in at the left cuff. The officer for this set was mounted and all the figures considerably larger than the normal size.

Other sets quickly followed this modest beginning. They included the famed Black Watch (the first in a line of popular kilted Highland regiments) running at the trail with rifles plugged in at the cuff (hence the "plug-handed Highlander"), several regiments of hussars, and the first line-infantry unit, the East Kent Regiment. This last regiment, nicknamed "The Buffs," set the pattern for other sets of line infantry; it contained 10 figures, including 7 soldiers at the ready, a boy drummer and bugler, and an officer.

Britains figures were generally made in what was termed "standard size"—54 millimeters or $2\frac{1}{8}$ inches—with mounted cavalry proportionately larger. This enabled a youngster to build a collection that was uniform in appearance. Furthermore, because Britains lead soldiers came in only a few basic positions—such as marching and running with rifles at the slope or the trail, standing and kneeling with bayonets fixed as if defending against cavalry, and charging—a young collector could build up formations of marching troops or the well-known British square of troops standing or kneeling at the ready, or firing from standing, kneeling, and lying positions—a defensive formation that had stopped Napoleon's heavy cavalry at Waterloo and the fanatical Dervishes in the Sudan.

Early sets were nicely packaged in long red boxes with a simple label on the lid containing the name of the regiment and the company trademark, originally given as "W. Britain." (More elaborate labels, featuring drawings of troops, regimental badges, and battleflags, were introduced later.) A standard box initially contained 10 infantry (reduced to 8 when movable arms were added) or 5 cavalry figures, although early in its history the company produced special display sets containing larger numbers of toy troops. The largest of these, Set Number 131, provided an array of 16 different British units and contained a total of 275 figures.

Despite every effort to make their line of toy soldiers commercially attractive, Britains figures did not achieve instant acceptance. Always slow to change, conservative London shopkeepers thought it prudent to stay with the better-known products of established German firms. Finally, William Britain persuaded the proprietors of Gamage's, one of London's most respected department stores, to take a few sets on a trial basis. Once on display, they were eagerly grabbed up by delighted young boys, and within a short time an entire department of Gamage's was devoted to the rapidly expanding line of hollow-cast toy soldiers by William Britain & Sons. Other shops quickly fell in step and the success of the firm's venture was assured.

The year 1895 saw Britains expand its line with a host of ambitious new sets that were to remain staple items in the catalogue throughout the years of lead soldier production. Among them were the first military musicians: the Band of the Line (Set No. 27), the Drums and Bugles of the Line (Set No. 30), and the Full Band of the Coldstream Guards (Set No. 37). The Band of the Line featured 12 figures with slotted arms (arms with pegs that could be inserted and then soldered into slots in the shoulders of the bandsmen); and the instruments included snare and bass drums, cornets, trombones, cymbals, fife, and a tubalike instrument called a bombardon. The Drums and Bugles of the Line, with fixed-arm buglers and drum major, originally sold at Gamage's for $10\frac{1}{2}$ pence (about 25 cents) and was quite popular. (In 1911 all of the band sets were altered to the movable-arm variety.)

The Band of the Coldstream Guards was the first in a long line of full (21-piece) band sets put out by the firm. Tradition has it that the choice of this regimental band was the result of circumstance. During the summer of 1895, the Coldstream Guards band performed in concert at Southend-on-Sea, which happened to be the hometown of William Britain, Jr. The younger Britain, after attending

Britains' first full musical corps was the Band of the Coldstream
Guards. Here we see the first version of that set, issued in 1895, with
half-booted bandsmen and slotted arms. Note in the rear the curved
tubalike instrument, called a bombardon.
Burtt Ehrlich Collection   Height: 54 mm

one of the concerts, decided that a miniature replica of the band would make a splendid offering for that year's Christmas trade and it was issued at that time. (However, this story is disputed by L. Dennis Britain, son of William, Jr., who claims the choice was randomly made.)

Branching out into other areas during this banner year, Britains put out the Mountain Battery of the Royal Artillery (Set No. 28), consisting of marching gunners and a mounted officer in foreign service helmets, four mules carrying the dismantled sections of a mountain gun, and a bundle of ammunition that could be shot out of the gun by means of a spring mechanism. Another artillery unit, the Royal Horse Artillery gun team (Set No. 39), with horses at the gallop, was also brought out in time for the Christmas season and sold for 2 shillings and 6 pence (about 75 cents). Early versions of this set, with gunners seated on the limber, are now extremely rare and command high prices at toy soldier auctions.

As a novelty item, in the tradition of its earlier mechanical toys, Britains put out a set of "Soldiers to Shoot" in 1895. This set featured four kneeling and firing line infantrymen with a catapult-like metal spring that, when bent and released, would propel a small bullet through the barrel of the rifle. These figures were produced for a relatively short period (from 1895 to 1914) and are now quite rare.

In anticipation of the forthcoming Diamond Jubilee, Britains began producing sets of soldiers from different parts of the empire. Colorfully garbed Indian Army regiments—including the 3rd Madras Cavalry and the 10th Bengal Lancers—made their appearance in 1896, along with the Egyptian Camel Corps (Set No. 48) and the South Australian Lancers (Set No. 49). These were followed by more Indian regiments—among them the 1st Madras Native Infantry (in scarlet tunics, turbans, and blue trousers), the 2nd Bombay Native Infantry and the 1st Bombay Lancers—the following year.

The year 1896 also saw the introduction of the first set with standard style movable arms, the 2nd Life Guards (Set No. 43), galloping with carbines in their hands. The arms were cast separately with a hole at the shoulder level, then pressed onto a peg jutting from the shoulder of the figure and painted into place. Infantry figures with movable arms were introduced in 1897 and older sets were gradually altered so that they, too, would have this popular feature, which served to further distinguish Britains' lead soldiers from those of European competitors.

With the coming of the campaign against the Dervishes in the Sudan and the Second Boer War, Britains became more topical. The charge of the 21st Lancers at the Battle of Omdurman (1898), in which a young subaltern named Winston Churchill participated, led to the issuance of a set of the 21st in khaki foreign-service uniforms and pith helmets just a few months after the battle. Boer cavalry and infantry (1899) were soon joined by other khaki-uniformed sets from that conflict, such as the Dublin Fusiliers and the Devonshire Regiments (1901). Similarly, the Russo-Japanese War (1904–5) resulted in a series of Russian and Japanese cavalry and infantry sets.

As war clouds gathered over the Balkans, Britains brought out boxes of Bulgarian, Serbian, and Montenegrin infantry (Set Nos. 172–74), along with Greek and Italian troops. In fact, beginning in 1904, when the Russian and Japanese sets (Nos. 133–36) were put out, there is a clear shift from a parochial emphasis on British troops to a more international perspective. More than half the new sets issued between 1904 and the beginning of World War I were of foreign units, mainly representing the nations—France, Germany, Italy, Austria, and the Balkan states—that would be participants in that conflict.

From the outset of its involvement in the production of toy soldiers, Britains made constant efforts to improve its figures. Anatomical anomalies and curious body postures that marred the first figures were gradually eliminated. Early horses, for example, had one ear instead of two, the assumption being that since the figure would normally be seen in profile it did not really matter. When equestrian purists complained, the "single-eared horse" was speedily replaced by one that was anatomically correct. Similarly, the first issue of the 5th and 9th Lancer regiments (1894)

(continued on page 126)

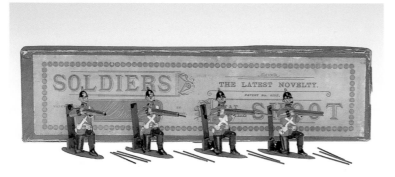

The earliest Britains infantry figures had fixed arms, which were changed later to the movable arms that became a trademark of the firm's toy soldier line. Above we see the first version of the Royal Sussex Regiment with the oval bases that were standard before 1906.
Burtt Ehrlich Collection   Height: 54 mm

An extremely rare Royal Field Artillery 10-horse gun team hitched up to an 18-inch howitzer.
Burtt Ehrlich Collection   Height: 70 mm

An early version of the King's Royal Rifle Corps, with a box bearing
a simple printed label giving the regiment's battle honors.
Burtt Ehrlich Collection   Height: 54 mm

Another early boxed Britains set, this one of the Somerset Light
Infantry; the original version featured eight standing and kneeling
soldiers, an officer, and a bugler. In later years the set was reduced
to seven soldiers and an officer with binoculars.
Burtt Ehrlich Collection   Height: 54 mm

The earliest Britains infantry figures had fixed arms, which were changed in 1896 to the movable arms that became a trademark of the firm's toy soldier line. Above we see the first version of the Royal Sussex Regiment with the oval bases that were standard before 1900.

Burtt Ehrlich Collection   Height: 54 mm

An excellent example of an early Britains Set No. 74, the Royal
Welch Fusiliers (second version, with oval bases and movable
arms), with an interesting, early illustrated box.
Burtt Ehrlich Collection   Height: 54 mm

The principal figures of a rare Britains set of "Soldiers on Parade" in its original display box.
Burtt Ehrlich Collection

Height: Foot figures: 54 mm
Mounted: 70 mm

The first version of the 11th Hussars, a well-known regiment
nicknamed "The Cherry Pickers." Note the throat plume on the
officer's prancing horse.
Burtt Ehrlich Collection   Height: 70 mm

At the time of Queen Victoria's Diamond Jubilee, Britains brought out a series of sets depicting troops of the British Empire. Among the Indian Army regiments was the 3rd Madras Light Cavalry, shown here against a backdrop of an early "Printer's Flowers" box.
Burtt Ehrlich Collection   Height: 70 mm

A close-up of the 2nd Bombay Native Infantry.
Burtt Ehrlich Collection   Height: 54 mm

Two versions of the Bikanir Camel Corps; an early version with a
wire-tailed camel and a detachable rider is on the right.
Burtt Ehrlich Collection   Height: 100 mm

An early version of Britains' West India Regiment with oval bases and mounted and foot officers.
Burtt Ehrlich Collection

Height: Foot figures: 54 mm
Mounted: 70 mm

The later, square-based version of the same set with a mounted officer on a straight-legged horse. Like many of the early sets, this one was discontinued after World War II.
Burtt Ehrlich Collection

Height: Foot figures: 54 mm
Mounted: 70 mm

had troopers mounted on a standing horse with oddly crossed rear legs. The "cross-legged" horse was quickly phased out, and the cast-lead lances carried by the troopers were replaced by a more realistic looking weapon made with a wire rod.

Curiosities also appeared—and disappeared—among the infantry figures. An early version of the Royal Fusiliers had an officer walking with his feet in a position similar to the hands of a clock at a quarter to three. In a later version, we find the officer's foot problem has been cured, and he is now marching in the proper heel-and-toe position. First-version line infantrymen running at the trail had an exaggerated barrel chest—the so-called "pigeon-chested" infantrymen. Eventually, they were slimmed down to a trimmer, more elegant looking specimen of British military manhood. Britains also took note of uniform and equipment changes and updated their figures accordingly. Half boots tucked into trousers gave way to full trouser legs; and adornments such as aiguillettes and campaign medals came off in conformance with new uniform regulations. Bases were originally round or oval and later became oblong or rectangular.

Although Britains made some improvements in the early years of production, the first truly "perfected," or anatomically correct, figures began to appear at the turn of the century, beginning with the issuance of the City Imperial Volunteers (Set No. 104) in 1900. The City Imperial Volunteers were also the first figures to bear a copyright label with the name of the manufacturer and the date of first issue of the particular model. Initially this information appeared on a small piece of paper attached under the base, but later it was engraved on the underside of the figure or base. By doing so, Britains hoped to gain protection, under the Sculpture Copyright Act of 1814, against pirate firms then engaged in putting out obvious copies of Britains figures—an indication, though an unhappy one, of the growing success of the company's products. (From 1900 to 1912, the copyright designation was "Copyright Wm Britain Jr," with the date of first issue and often the words "Made in England." Beginning in

1913, the designation was changed to "Britains Ltd. Copyright. Proprietors.")

Because the early imperfect models had such short lives, they are now quite scarce and are eagerly sought after by sophisticated collectors of what are called "ancient Britains." (The term is generally used as a designation for all the models produced by Britains before World War I.) The serious collector usually will try to obtain examples of the different variations or "versions" of a particular set. For example, he might want a first version of the Mountain Artillery (Set No. 28) with the smaller-than-standard-size walking gunners on oval bases, mules with bent legs, and a fixed-arm officer on a walking horse; a later version with the gunners, still short, on square bases and the mules with straighter legs; and the final version, with taller gunners on square bases and an officer with movable arms on a trotting horse. Such attention to subtle variations is the hallmark of the connoisseur collector and explains why complete sets of "ancient Britains" may sell—depending on condition and whether they are boxed or unboxed—for $300 to $1,000 and sometimes much more.

Whatever the version or period, Britains figures are always distinguishable by the formality of pose. The toy soldiers of Messrs. Britain are never portrayed lounging about campfires or casually positioned. Whether marching, running, walking, or charging, they are almost always ramrod straight. Even charging cavalrymen are not hunched over their horses' necks as they might be in a real charge; they are bolt upright in the saddle as if on parade. No doubt the influence of late-19th-century military artists such as Richard Simkin was at work here. Many early Britains models were clearly inspired by Simkin prints, then appearing with regularity in the *Army and Navy Gazette*. Simkin depicted his British troops in an idealized fashion that emphasized proper uniform and correct bearing.

Although most Britains figures were made in the standard 54-millimeter size, the company did produce both smaller and larger models. In 1896, Britains intro-

(continued on page 160)

During the first twenty years of production, Britains improved the anatomy of its models. The first "perfected" figures were those representing the City Imperial Volunteers. Issued in 1900, these figures were also the first to carry a copyright designation under the bases, which became necessary because of the activities of pirate firms.

Burtt Ehrlich Collection

Height: 70 mm

Another popular Britains set was the Royal Artillery Mountain Battery. The earliest version of this set featured smaller-than-standard-size gunners on oval bases, mules with bent legs and longer ears than later versions, and a fixed-arm mounted officer.
Burtt Ehrlich Collection   Height: Foot figures: 54 mm
                                                              Mounted: 70 mm

Here we have the later version of the same set, with larger, standard-sized gunners, straight-legged mules, and a movable-arm officer mounted on a sturdier trotting horse.
Burtt Ehrlich Collection   Height: Foot figures: 54 mm
                                                              Mounted: 70 mm

PRINCIPAL ORDNANCE OFFICER.
PRINCIPAL MEDICAL OFFICER.

GENERAL STAFF.

AIDE DE CAMP.   PRINCIPAL ROYAL ENGINEER   PRINCIPAL ROYAL ARTILLERY OFFICER.   DIRECTOR-GENERAL.
(Colonel on the Staff.)   FIELD-MARSHAL.   (Colonel on the Staff.) LIEUTENANT-GENERAL.   COLONEL ON THE STAFF.   Army Veterinary Department.

STAFF.

THE NEW SERVICE DRESS FOR BRITISH OFFICERS.

ROYAL FIELD ARTILLERY.   ROYAL ENGINEERS.   INFANTRY OF THE LINE.   CAVALRY.   ARMY SERVICE CORPS.
Lieutenant.   Captain.   Lieutenant.   Captain.   Major.   Captain.
(Foreign Service Hat.)   (Foreign Service Hat.)

VOLUNTEER ROYAL ARTILLERY.

OFFICER.   FIELD-OFFICER.   OFFICER.   16 POUNDER RIFLED MUZZLE-LOADING FIELD GUN AND DETACHMENT.
Undress.   Review Order.   Review Order.

Supplement to THE ARMY & NAVY GAZETTE. Saturday, December 3, 1898.

MILITARY TYPES—No. 198.

THE WEST INDIA REGIMENT.

The military prints of artist Richard Simkin, with their formally posed British and colonial troops, served as inspiration for many of the early Britains sets.

In this early version of the 5th Royal Irish Lancers, we see one of
Britains' most striking figures, that of an officer turned in the saddle.
The figure was based on a print by military artist Richard Simkin,
whose artwork served as inspiration for many Britains models.
Burtt Ehrlich Collection   Height: 70 mm

Although its 54mm figures were the most popular and widely
distributed, Britains also issued a range of smaller-size (45mm)
figures originally designated the "B" Series. Here we see a unit of
the Royal Horse Artillery in the active-service dress uniforms worn
during the Boer War.
Burtt Ehrlich Collection   Height: 60 mm

The first version of the Band of the Life Guards, with slotted arms
and the old bombardon, later replaced by the modern tuba.
Burtt Ehrlich Collection   Height: 70 mm

Extremely rare, because of its short duration in the catalogue, is the
band of another Household Cavalry regiment, the Royal Horse
Guards ("The Blues").
Burtt Ehrlich Collection   Height: 70 mm

"Colours and Pioneers of the Scots Guards," showing an early
version with full equipment, oval bases, and a flag-bearer with
a flat flag, and the later version, square-based with a color-bearer
holding a partly furled flag.
Burtt Ehrlich Collection   Height: 70 mm

A rare Britains Ltd Display Set # 73 (Royal Artillery Gun Team not
illustrated), an early version slotted-arm Band of the Line,
Highlanders, Lancers and Royal Fusiliers.

Photo courtesy of Phillips, New York.

Horse-drawn artillery units were enormously popular and, in 1895, Britains issued the first of many versions of the Royal Horse Artillery gun team with gunners seated on the limber and on bucket seats on the cannon.
Burtt Ehrlich Collection   Height: Mounted figures: 70 mm

A later version of the Royal Horse Artillery in its original box.
Burtt Ehrlich Collection   Height: 70 mm

An extremely rare Britains Set # 318, Royal Horse Artillery Gun Team at the halt in active service order, with six-horse team, three drivers, gun, limber, mounted officer and team of standing and kneeling gunners with standing officer holding binoculars (16-piece version, as issued). Sold with original box designated "Royal Horse Artillery review order" in 1987 for $8,500.

Photo courtesy of Phillips, New York.

Over the years many variations of the Royal Horse Artillery were
produced by Britains, including this rare version with the gunners in
steel helmets.
Burtt Ehrlich Collection   Height: 70 mm

A first-version set of the Royal Field Artillery in review order
showing the horses with collar harnesses and the gunners seated on
the limber and the cannon.
Burtt Ehrlich Collection   Height: 70 mm

The British campaign in the Sudan prompted the issuance of
Egyptian troops such as this Egyptian Camel Corps unit.
Burtt Ehrlich Collection   Height: Camel: 75 mm

Egyptian cavalry in a Whisstock box.
Burtt Ehrlich Collection   Height: Mounted: 65 mm

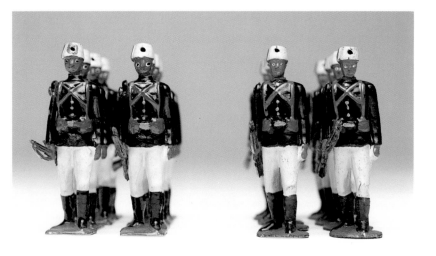

A column of Sudanese troops like those who served with British
forces in the Sudan campaign of the late 1890s.
Burtt Ehrlich Collection   Height: 54 mm

Fighting alongside the Sudanese would have been these Britains
Egyptian infantrymen, shown here in two versions, the earlier (left),
with oval bases and paper labels with copyright information
underneath the bases, and the later square-based version at right.
Burtt Ehrlich Collection   Height: 54 mm

The successful British military campaign in 1898 against the
Dervishes in the Sudan prompted the issuance of the 21st Lancers in
their foreign-service uniforms. This regiment earned renown for its
gallant charge at the Battle of Omdurman.
Burtt Ehrlich Collection   Height: 70 mm

Many versions of the 21st Lancers were issued, showing them in
both review order and active-service uniforms. Here we see a
variation in World War I-period steel helmets.
Burtt Ehrlich Collection   Height: 70 mm

The first version of the South Australian Lancers, showing them in
bush hats.
Burtt Ehrlich Collection   Height: 70 mm

A detail of the later version of the South Australian Lancers, with the
troopers in khaki service uniforms and spiked pith helmets.
Burtt Ehrlich Collection   Height: 70 mm

Britains' first set of foreign troops was of Boer infantry, which were
first issued at the time of the Second Boer War.
Burtt Ehrlich Collection   Height: 54 mm

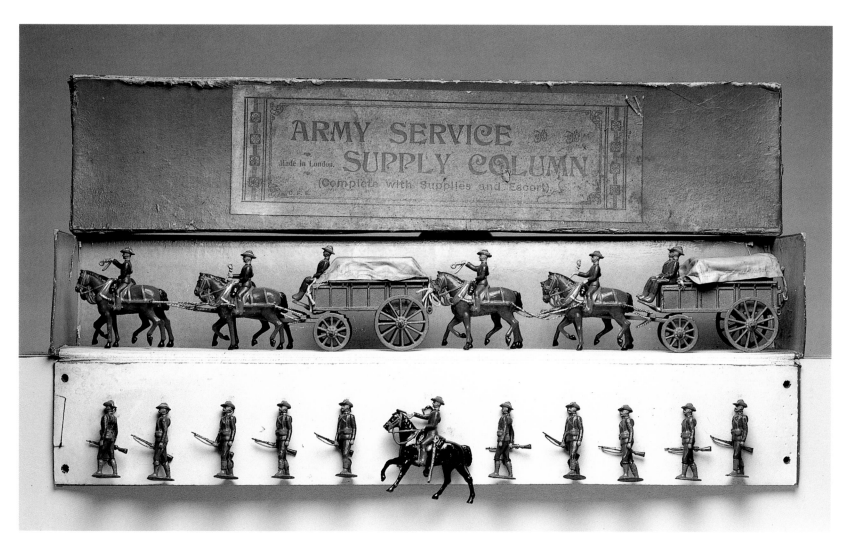

This Boer War–period Army Service Supply Column, including horse-drawn wagons and an escort of Imperial Yeomen, was produced by Britains but sold under another label (CFE). A set recently sold at Phillips for $11,000—a record price for a toy soldier lot in the U.S.

Burtt Ehrlich Collection

Height: Foot figures: 54 mm
Mounted: 70 mm

During the Russo-Japanese War, Britains produced sets of Russian
and Japanese infantry. Here we see a rare version of Japanese
infantry marching at the slope with a mounted officer.
Burtt Ehrlich Collection   Height: Foot figures: 54 mm
                                                           Mounted: 70 mm

A more common version of Japanese infantry charging.
Burtt Ehrlich Collection   Height: 54 mm

Three versions of Japanese cavalry, showing them both in light-blue
uniform coats and in the rarer and accurate dark-blue uniform coats.
Burtt Ehrlich Collection   Height: 70 mm

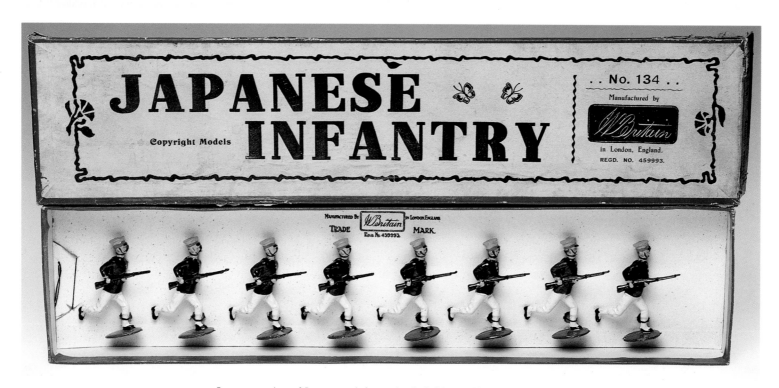

A rare version of Japanese infantry in dark-blue uniform coats,
issued only briefly.
Burtt Ehrlich Collection   Height: 54 mm

In the years just before World War I, Britains brought out sets of troops representing the various Balkan states. Here we see an early version of Serbian infantry with its "Printer's Flowers" box.

Height: 54 mm

Two versions of Montenegrin infantry, with the early model marching at the slope.
Burtt Ehrlich Collection

Height: 54 mm

The first "pigeon-chested" version of Greek infantry running at the trail.
Burtt Ehrlich Collection   Height: 54 mm

A detachment of Greek cavalry by Britains.
Burtt Ehrlich Collection   Height: 70 mm

Britains produced few sets of German troops: the earliest was of
Prussian infantry in their familiar *pickelhaube* (spiked) helmets.
Burtt Ehrlich Collection   Height: 54 mm

Now extremely rare, this set of Prussian hussars was produced
before World War I.
Burtt Ehrlich Collection   Height: 70 mm

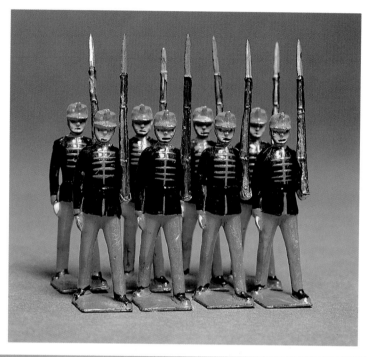

Britains turned out soldiers of the major combatants in World War I. Troops of the Austro-Hungarian Army included these colorful Infantry of the Line.
Burtt Ehrlich Collection
Height: 54 mm

Although designated as lancers, these rare Austro-Hungarian cavalrymen carry swords.
Burtt Ehrlich Collection
Height: 70 mm

TYPES OF THE AUSTRO-HUNGARIAN ARMY.

Copyright Models
by
Wm. Britain, Jun.

Lancers

Manufactured by

W. Britain

in London, England.

The French Army was well represented in Britains' catalogues. This
rare version of French line infantry turned out by the Paris office
included a standard-bearer and a mounted officer.
Burtt Ehrlich Collection   Height: 54 mm

Much sought after and hard to find is this Britains set of French
Chasseurs à Cheval, decked out in their full plumage.
Burtt Ehrlich Collection

Height: 70 mm

A rare group of French Army dragoons on parade.
Burtt Ehrlich Collection   Height: 54 mm

duced some 70-millimeter figures (designated as the "H" range) and a series of 45-millimeter figures (subsequently designated the "B" series) that were produced under the same demanding standards as their top-grade 54-millimeter figures. Later, in 1905, the company added an "A" and "X" series of 54-millimeter figures made from earlier fixed-arm molds that had since been updated. Painted as second-grade figures, they represented an attempt to appeal to prospective customers who could not afford the better-quality models. They are generally only of passing interest to today's collectors.

The expansion of Britains Ltd., the name adopted in 1907, when the British "Company Act" was introduced, continued steadily throughout the first decade of the 20th century. A French subsidiary was opened in 1905, which, in addition to the general range of toy soldiers, also produced some sets intended exclusively for the French market. Figures produced by the French branch of Britains bear the further designation "Déposé" under the base. By this time, Britains had all but swept its German competitors from the domestic field. To further promote its lead soldiers, the company put out, in 1908, a delightful booklet entitled *The Great War Game for Young and Old*, which used photographs of actual troops as well as Britains lead soldiers to illustrate how war games ought to be conducted. The Britains book, which is now known to

have been written by H. G. Wells, probably inspired him to write *Floor Games*, published in 1911, and his later and more famous *Little Wars*.

Britains steadily added to its premier line of 54-millimeter figures, and the total number of different sets rose from 126 in 1901 to more than 200 numbered sets at the outbreak of World War I. At that time, the company drastically curtailed its production of toy soldiers and began to manufacture munitions in order to aid the war effort. By then, Britains was already exporting hundreds of thousands of boxed sets of lead soldiers to Europe and the United States. There must have been a special sense of satisfaction in the fact that large numbers of the firm's figures were being imported into Germany, and that the firm of Georg Heyde, their chief rival, was now producing a line of hollow-cast figures imitative of their own, and referred to by Heyde as "toy soldiers made in the English manner."

Indeed, the firm could accurately boast, as it did in an early post–World War I catalogue, that Britains had successfully cracked what had been "exclusively a German industry," and that they had "converted the old saying 'British Soldiers made in Germany' not only to 'British Soldiers made in Britain,' but before the Great War were actually supplying the German market with 'German Soldiers made in England.'"

Peacetime Pursuits

Following the armistice of 1918, Britains swung back into full-scale production. Initially, the firm added to the ranks of its military line, but it soon became obvious that the public's enthusiasm for toy warriors had been considerably diminished by the horrors of real war. The incredible carnage of the Somme, Passchendaele, and Third Ypres—where each square mile of territory gained in five months of fighting had cost the British more than 8,000 men—had not left much to cheer about, even in victory. There was, after all, little glory in a war that saw armies herded behind barbed-wire enclosures where, as Major General J. F. C. Fuller put it, they were "reduced to the position of human cattle."

The natural consequence of this unparalleled bloodletting was an upsurge of antiwar sentiment and a temporary move toward arms control. Mindful of the public mood, Britains joined the pacifist parade, literally beating its swords into plowshares. In the early 1920s, the company brought out its "Model Home Farm" series. Early models were a predictable mix of common farm animals—horses, cows, sheep, pigs, and the like—farmers and their wives, and an assortment of country village and farm folk. Immediately successful, the farm range was steadily expanded over the next decade, so that by the mid-1930s there were more than 200 separate entries in the section of the catalogue devoted to this series.

Indeed, the "Model Home Farm" series eventually offered a youngster almost every type of model his fanciful mind could conjure up. Horse-drawn plows, farm wagons, and rakes lumbered across make-believe fields or down imaginary country lanes flanked by rail fences or flint walls (available at 3 pence for each section); blacksmiths hammered out horseshoes on anvils; shepherds tended

their flocks; children played on seesaws or garden swings; and a host of farmhands—among them navvies with picks and shovels, stable boys, and milkmaids—performed their various tasks. Cottages, too, could be had, with imitation thatched roofs "constructed in one piece, of a special composition, without nails or glue. No joints to come apart. No rough edges to scratch or cause damage." And villagers galore: old folks sitting on benches; curates and country clergymen; milkmen and policemen; a family off to a Sunday outing on a motorcycle with sidecar; and a golfer striding toward the green, clutching his club. Not to mention such charming touches as "Dog, begging" and a "Spiteful cat" (Nos. 637 and 638 in the catalogue, only 1 pence each).

Most of the farm items were sold individually from counter display boxes; but there were also boxed sets with different assortments of animals, farm people, and various shrubs and trees. One attractive display box came with a foldout scenic backdrop showing a farmhouse and rustic bridge. Britains proudly displayed their ever-expanding farm series at the annual British Industries Fair and other exhibitions. It was at one of these yearly expositions that a member of the royal family, after favorably commenting on the completeness of the Britains display, casually remarked that the only thing lacking was a village idiot. The royal aside was Britains' command, and the following year saw the deficiency corrected: a village idiot was added to the "Model Home Farm" exhibit.

The farm series retained its popularity until the end of Britains' metal production, its success no doubt aided by its appeal to both young boys and girls and older family members. "It is just that kind of toy which can be played with equally well by the youngest or oldest child, not to

One of the earliest civilian groups produced by Britains was this charming Victorian family said to have been based on Fred Britain's family.
Burtt Ehrlich Collection   Height: 60 mm

Reacting to antiwar sentiment, Britains greatly expanded its civilian ranges during the 1920s and 1930s. Especially popular was its "Model Home Farm" series, which included the six-wheeled dump truck and barn shown above.
Burtt Ehrlich Collection

A convoy of Britains military vehicles, including open and covered army lorries, passes through an English country village made up of Britains civilian houses from its "Model Home Farm" range.
Burtt Ehrlich Collection

When a member of the royal
family commented that only a
village idiot was missing from an
impressive Britains farm display,
the company quickly issued a
figure to correct this deficiency.
Burtt Ehrlich Collection
                    Height: 54 mm

METAL SOLDIERS
AND TOYS

Manufactured by
BRITAINS LIMITED, LONDON, ENGLAND.

BRITISH INDUSTRIES FAIR, 1922.

**His Majesty King George V.
inspects his armies in miniature**

WHEN BUYING BRITAINS SOLDIERS SEE THAT THEY ARE BRITAINS

In the late 1930s, Britains issued an attractive display of Noah's Ark.
The ark was made of cardboard and the animals and figures of Noah
and his wife were derived from existing models.
Burtt Ehrlich Collection

mention a large number of grown-ups," stated a 1930s promotional blurb, "and the fact that it can be added to at will, and is so infinitely varied, ensures that there is never any likelihood of its failing to give pleasure to even the most changeable youngster, and mother or father may be sure of quiet evenings if Britains' 'Model Home Farm' is in the home."

Success with the farm figures led to other nonmilitary lines. A zoological series offering a variety of animals "majestic, ferocious, or docile as the case may be" was begun in the early 1930s. To capture what it termed "that indefinable attraction of the wild," Britains issued nearly 100 different models of wild animals, from bears and bison to tortoises and tapirs. Many of the figures were designed by L. D. (Dennis) Britain, who had succeeded his father, William Britain, Jr., as a director of the firm and one of its principal modelers. Certain animals, among them hippos, rhinos, and elephants, apparently held a special attraction and were offered at various stages of life. Thus we have a fully grown adult rhinoceros, a young rhino, and a baby, described in the catalogue as "a true chip off the old block, down to armour plating and horn."

In a truly educational spirit, Britains catalogue descriptions provided the Latin name of the animal and a brief description of its peculiar characteristics. Thus we learn that *Phacochoerus aethiopicus* (or wart hog if you prefer) "is the ugliest member of the Hog family, and probably the most powerful"; and that the towering *Giraffa camelopardalis* (the giraffe) has to spread-eagle its front legs "in order to pick up anything from the ground." Fencing, zookeepers, and palm trees completed the tabletop zoo; and an "Elephant Ride," with Indian elephant, howdah, and two children as passengers, duplicated in miniature a popular attraction at the London Zoological Gardens. Shortly before World War II, a "Noah's Ark" set was added to the series, comprising a cardboard ark, Noah and his wife, and a proper assortment of animals in pairs.

The English love of gardens is well known and Britains accommodated this botanical interest with its "Miniature Gardening Series." Intended almost exclusively for the home market, the series featured a rich selection of shrubs, plants, flowers, and flower beds. Then, too, there were rockeries, greenhouses, sundials, and lily ponds. Naturally, gardeners with rollers and lawn mowers were on hand to keep the grounds tidy and trim. As with other series, Britains promoted its miniature gardens both as children's toys and as models for adults; and it was asserted that "the gardener, amateur or professional [could] plan out his garden in a thoroughly practical manner . . . arranging and re-arranging his design in miniature until a satisfactory one has been reached."

One of the most delightful of the civilian lines was Britain's "Mammoth Circus." Some of the firm's most unusual and best-designed models were here to be found. Though not as richly varied as Mignot's circus range, there was a good mix of big-top performers and trained animals: clowns in baggy pants or twirling a hoop while perched atop a prancing horse; men on stilts; a ringmaster with whip handling show horses balanced on their rear legs; and a delicate figure of an equestrienne in ballet pose who could stand gracefully on the back of a horse or an elephant. All figures were available individually or in several boxed combinations. To these were added a roundabout, or merry-go-round, that could be made to spin around by a flick of the fingers, and a "flying trapeze," a mechanical toy in the old Britains tradition, consisting of a clown with an umbrella and a "fairy" perched on a trapeze, constructed so that as the duo moved across a stretched wire the umbrella would twirl.

Just about all facets of life as it was then known could be found in Britains' civilian lines. Formally garbed hunters and huntswomen chased after the wily fox accompanied by a pack of hounds and handlers; and there were English footballers in boxed sets representing the major British teams. (If your favorite team was not already in stock, Britains would paint standard figures to order in appropriate colors.) A popular "Motor and Road'" series featured attractive models of an open touring car (which

As part of its "Miniature Gardens," Britains turned out an assortment
of gnomes in various sizes and postures. Some of them are seen
above with a Britains farmhouse in the background.
Burtt Ehrlich Collection

Extremely popular among children was Britains' "Mammoth Circus,"
with its show horses, clowns, a man on stilts, a boxing kangaroo, and
an assortment of circus animals.
Burtt Ehrlich Collection

doubled as a police car), a two-seater coupé model with fitted bumpers, and a dashing, streamlined "Blue Bird" racing car. There were jockeys on race horses with—unusual for Britains—detachable riders painted in the colors of famous owners such as Lord Astor and the Aga Khan, and a popular series of railway-station figures to accompany 1-gauge toy trains. In short, with a proper selection of Britains models, a youngster could create his own world in miniature.

From the mid-1930s on, the firm added a range of novelty items that included miniature household utensils, decorative Christmas tree ornaments, and such incidentals as gnomes in various poses, and a bird warbler guaranteed to reproduce the notes of song birds—"No skill required." The popularity of Walt Disney cartoon characters prompted Britains to issue, from 1939 to 1941, a small series of the better known of these. Mickey Mouse was represented, along with his friends Minnie, Donald Duck, Pluto, Clarabelle, and Goofy, all with a new twist, so to speak—movable heads. This was followed by Snow White and her entourage of seven dwarfs, each figure a recognizable likeness of the well-known crew: Doc, Dopey, Sleepy, Sneezy, Happy, Bashful, and Grumpy. Britains even briefly turned futuristic with a group of figures depicting the major characters from the "Buck Rogers" comic strip begun in 1929. Armed with an XZ–31 rocket pistol, Buck and his female sidekick, Wilma Deering, were ready to do battle against the evil Killer Kane and his cronies in crime. In all, there were six figures in the series; they were sold in the United States through retail outlets and also were given as a radio premium in exchange for three boxtops from a popular breakfast cereal plus 50 cents. A point of interest is that, unlike other Britains figures produced between 1924 and 1937, they do not bear the standard copyright designation "Britains Ltd., Copyright, Proprietors, Made in England" under the bases. Instead, they are marked "Made in England, J. Dille & Co."—John Dille being the newspaper syndicate president who commissioned the original comic strip, and who held exclusive rights for licensing Buck Rogers toys

and novelties.

The extent to which Britains had moved into civilian lines is easily gauged by a comparison of the pre–World War I situation with that of the interwar years. Before 1914, fewer than ten civilian sets (excluding pistol-packing "North American Cowboys") were available—among them Salvation Army bandsmen and personnel, Boy Scouts, and railway figures—while in the 1930s there were several hundred. In fact, nearly two-thirds of Britains' catalogues from 1936 to 1939 were devoted to nonmilitary items.

Be that as it may, military themes were not being ignored during these years of growth. Many of the new military models resulted from burgeoning overseas sales. Although the Paris branch was closed down in 1923, due to operational difficulties, Britains discovered fertile ground in the New World. A serious effort to exploit the American market began in the early 1920s with the issuance of United States and Latin American military models. The Argentines and Uruguayans were represented by a colorful array of infantry, cavalry, and military school cadets in review order. (Mexico was already in the catalogue with a single infantry set, "Rurales de la Federación," decked out in sombreros.) By design or oversight, Britains had limited their range of United States soldiers to just two sets before the Great War. This was remedied in 1924 with a small deluge of United States cavalry, Marines, and natty West Point cadets in dress uniforms. Subsequent years saw a myriad of display-set variations employing these basic models. New figures also appeared on a regular basis: sailors, both in blue and white uniforms, machine gunners, and infantry in battle dress with gas masks. There was also a khaki-clad military band, available in either a 12- or a 21-piece set, based on a similarly attired British Army band and distinguished from the latter by subtle variations in painting (black shoes for the British, brown for the Americans).

An interesting group of "U. S. Aviation" sets came out in 1929, worth mentioning because new figures were created for them. In all, there were five sets: two of offi-

(continued on page 180)

Just about every facet of civilian life was covered by Britains. Soccer being an extremely popular sport, the firm issued figures painted to represent various British city teams.
Burtt Ehrlich Collection   Height: 54 mm

In the tradition of its earlier mechanical toys, Britains put out a "flying trapeze." When the clown and the "fairy" moved across an extended wire, the clown's umbrella would twirl.
Burtt Ehrlich Collection   Height: 54 mm

Another popular civilian toy was Britains' roundabout, which could be made to spin with a flick of the fingers.
Burtt Ehrlich Collection   Diameter: 5½ in.
                                            Height: 8 in.

A boxed set of Britains Girl Guides.
Height: 54 mm

Before World War I, Britains issued few civilian figures: among them were Boy Scouts marching and performing various chores.
Burtt Ehrlich Collection
Height: 54 mm

Another popular civilian range was the "Motor and Road" series, which included a two-seater coupé model and a police car with two policemen.

Length: Coupé: 4½ in. × 1¾ in.
Police car: 4½ in.

The "Motor and Road" series featured a futuristic-looking model of a "Blue Bird" racing car.
Burtt Ehrlich Collection

Length: 6⅜ in. (162 mm)

A Britains light goods van from its "Motor and Road" series.
Burtt Ehrlich Collection

A salesman's sample set of riders and horses from Britains "Jockey"
series; the jockeys wear the racing colors of various owners.
Burtt Ehrlich Collection   Height: Mounted jockey: 110 mm

The popularity of Walt Disney's cartoon characters led Britains to
issue a series of these, including Mickey Mouse, Donald Duck, Pluto,
Clarabelle, and others.
Burtt Ehrlich Collection

Britains turned futuristic in the 1930s, when the firm brought out
figures depicting characters from the "Buck Rogers" comic strip. The
figures were made for sale in the United States under the copyright
of John Dille, who commissioned the original comic strip in the
1920s.
Burtt Ehrlich Collection   Height: 54 mm

Snow White stands in the doorway of a farm cottage made for
Britains by Hugar while the Seven Dwarfs get ready for the day's
activities.
Burtt Ehrlich Collection

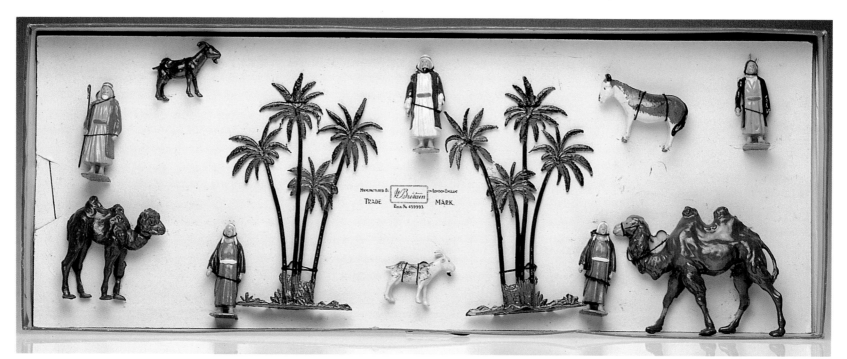

A rare set of "Eastern Peoples," first issued in the 1930s. Seen here is the postwar version.
Burtt Ehrlich Collection

Britains produced a group of personality
figures, such as Little Red Riding Hood, for
Madame Tussaud's Wax Museum.
Burtt Ehrlich Collection   Height: 65 mm

Britains produced souvenir models, such as these 65mm figures of
Henry VIII and Elizabeth I, for Madame Tussaud's Wax Museum.

cers (one group in short coats, the other in overcoats), one set of marching privates, and two of aviators in flying kit. Of special interest are the aviators. One wore a jacket with fur collar, baggy pants, and puttees. The other, standing with left hand on hip, was dressed in a more up-to-date Sidcot flying suit, a one-piece neck-to-ankle garment with pockets on the front of the trouser legs. Both pilots wore aviator caps with goggles raised over the forehead. Not long after, Britains added its first aircraft, a monoplane, which could be had with either R.A.F. or U.S. Army Air Corps markings. (The monoplane came in a special box that could be refolded to form a hangar for the plane.)

By the mid-1930s, Britains had fleshed out its United States military line to more than 50 sets, including two massive display boxes (Set Nos. 323 and 324) containing 73 and 81 pieces respectively. To these one might add two dozen sets of North American cowboys and Indians, and several sets of Girl Scouts and Boy Scouts, making the United States second only to Great Britain in the number of listings in the English toy firm's catalogue.

The British Army also received its full share of attention during these years. Popular service units like the Guards and certain of the other infantry and cavalry regiments were updated or issued in dress and pose variations—for example, the Grenadier Guards in winter coats and the Life Guards in their cold-weather scarlet cloaks. Greater attention was paid to support units, such as the Royal Army Service Corps and the Royal Engineers; there were horse-drawn limbered wagons in khaki service order and full dress; and a splendid Royal Engineers Pontoon Section with horse-drawn wagon, pontoon boat, and planking to form a bridge. Similarly, the Royal Horse and Royal Field Artillery gun teams, great favorites with youngsters, now appeared in a new variation, standing at the halt. Set Number 318 featured a team of gunners in active-service dress along with Britains' standard Gun of the Royal Artillery (Model 1201) and a standing horse team and limber. (In 1986, one of these extremely rare sets was sold at auction by Phillips, New York, for $8,500, one of the highest sums ever paid for a single lot of toy soldiers.)

Parades and processions being such an important part of playing with toy soldiers, Britains saw to it that there were bands galore for any military pageant. A 17-piece Drum and Fife Band of the Line (Set No. 321) appeared in 1929, along with a companion fife and drum corps of the Coldstream Guards (Set No. 322), which included a marching contingent of guardsmen. Later came a particularly colorful Band of the Royal Marines in their striking blue uniforms trimmed in red and topped by a white pith helmet, and a full-dress Band of the Royal Air Force, both available in 12- or 21-piece versions. The skirl of the bagpipes received full tribute with the issuance, in 1939, of Set Number 1722, Drum and Pipe Band of the Scots Guard, with a full complement of 12 pipers, 5 side drummers, bass drummer, cymbalist, and drum major. That same year, Britains brought out the Full Band of the Royal Scots Greys, the first mounted musicians produced by the firm since the original Household Cavalry bands had been turned out years earlier. (It was also the company's last mounted musical corps.) The full band consisted of 11 musicians and could be had for 7 shillings and 6 pence; while a smaller 7-piece version was priced at 4 shillings and 6 pence.

Most of the Britains bands became permanent fixtures in the catalogue and were revived after World War II. One that was not so favored was the 21-piece Band of the Royal Marine Light Infantry (Set No. 1622), which made its first appearance in 1938 and was withdrawn from the list a year later. Essentially the same composition as the standard Royal Marine band, its only distinguishable feature was the scarlet jackets worn by the musicians. Perhaps that lack of originality accounts for its failure to catch the public fancy and for Britains' decision to discontinue it. As a result of its short duration, it has become an exceptionally rare item. In 1977, an example of this set from the collection of actor Douglas Fairbanks, Jr., fetched what was then a record price for a single lot of toy soldiers

(continued on page 188)

At the time of the Spanish-American War, Britains issued its first sets of United States troops. The early versions of U. S. infantry were marching at the slope in campaign service dress. The two versions shown in the photograph are distinguishable only by painting variations and the fact that the officer belonging to the set on the left does not have a movable arm.
Burtt Ehrlich Collection   Height: 54 mm

Britains greatly expanded its range of U.S. soldiers after
World War I. Left, we see a group of doughboys

Part of a set of U.S. infantry in World War I uniforms, with a
box bearing a simple printed label.
Burtt Ehrlich Collection   Height: 54 mm

Britains produced West Point cadets in summer dress (left) and
winter dress.
Burtt Ehrlich Collection   Height: 54 mm

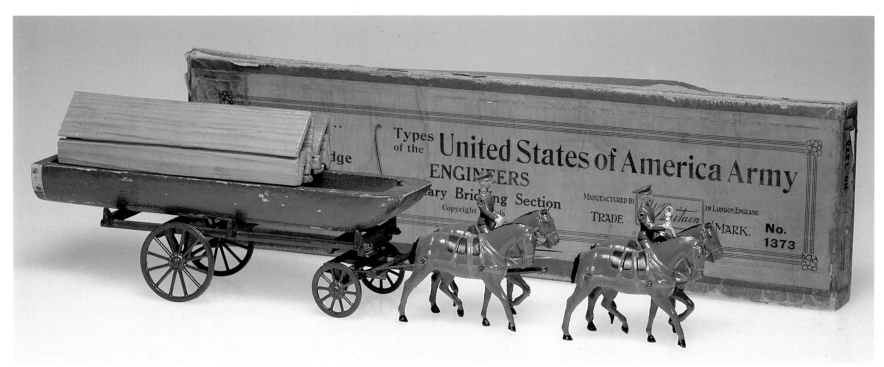

With a few simple brushstrokes, Britains was able to convert its
Royal Engineers Pontoon Bridging Section into a U.S. Army pontoon
section.
Burtt Ehrlich Collection

This rare Britains set of North American cowboys and Indians, complete with scenic backdrop, was made for distribution by the American Soldier Company.
Burtt Ehrlich Collection   Height: 54 mm

A war party of North American Indians by Britains is chased off by troops protecting a frontier fort.
Burtt Ehrlich Collection   Height: Foot figures: 54 mm
                                                      Mounted: 70 mm

Royal Canadian Mounted Policemen in winter dress form up in front of their frontier fort.
Burtt Ehrlich Collection   Height: 54 mm

when it was sold at a London saleroom of Phillips, the fine-art auctioneers. The event was reported by the *New York Times* in a two-column article that appeared under the headline "21 Toy Soldiers Auctioned for $1,392" in the paper's September 21, 1977, edition. The *Times* article, which sparked renewed interest in old toy soldiers as valuable collectibles, pointed out that "In 1938, when the figures . . . were made, they cost $1.50 a set." (More recently, in May 1986, a similar set was sold at a Phillips, New York, lead soldier auction for $4,800.)

In the 1930s, Britains, in an uncharacteristic gesture to the past, issued a small series of historical sets. The first of these was Set Number 1257, Beefeaters (Yeomen of the Guard), in their traditional Tudor-style uniforms; and Set Number 1258, Knights in Armour, a nice display featuring two mounted knights in tournament trappings, two squires holding pennons, a herald trumpeter sounding a call, and a marshal on horseback. The coronation of King George VI in 1937 produced a flurry of historical types, chief among them being a fine model of the State Coach of England, and figures of outriders, attendants, and footmen of the royal household to accompany it. Set Number 1477, a 75-piece display, was described as "A presentation box containing the State Coach of England and sufficient attendants, outriders, Footmen, Yeomen of the Guard, Staff Officers, Guards (mounted and dismounted) and Police, to make up a complete procession, as for the opening of Parliament. . . ." In line with the coronation celebration, Britains undertook to produce a complete series of the regiments of the British Regular Army, some 45 in all, using its basic marching line-infantry figure in full dress, with appropriate regimental facings. But, states one source, "It is doubtful if the project was a success for by 1940 none of the boxes remained on the list."

In 1937, the Royal United Services Museum had on display an exhibit of French troops of the Napoleonic Wars, using Lucotte and Mignot figures. Because there were no comparable toy soldiers of British troops of that period by a domestic maker, members of the British Model Soldier Society petitioned Britains to fill the gap.

The firm was agreeable and, in short order, turned out four sets of "Waterloo Period" line infantry and Highlanders. The troops wore full packs and carried either pikes or muskets at the shoulder arms position.

The Changing of the Guard at Buckingham Palace has long been one of London's top tourist attractions, and when Britains finally got around to creating a miniature version of this ceremony, they did it in fine style. First issued in 1937, Set Number 1555 was a massive two-tray display box measuring 22 by 13 inches and containing 83 pieces. Inside were troops of the Coldstream and Scots Guards, marching and at present arms, a full Band of the Coldstream Guards, color-bearers, officers, and sentry boxes—providing all of the ingredients for a youngster to faithfully reenact guard mount at the royal residence. It was reissued after the war and remained in the catalogue until the last years of lead soldier production.

Britains also followed the march of current history. When the Fascist forces of Benito Mussolini swept into Ethiopia in 1935, Britains quickly brought out toy troops representing the rival forces. According to L. W. Richards, "The Italian Government, in order to extol the strength of their armed forces, issued a book containing many coloured plates. Britains made use of these pictures when modeling the Italian figures." The new Italian sets included green-uniformed infantry in steel helmets, tunics opened at the neck to reveal the black shirts that were a synonym for Italian Fascists; colonial infantry in light-colored tropical uniforms and pith helmets; and the Carabinieri, Italy's elite paramilitary police force, in full ceremonial splendor. Against them were arrayed white-robed Ethiopian tribesmen and a barefoot bodyguard of the emperor of Abyssinia in pale-green dress uniforms with peaked caps and epaulets.

Regardless of period or type, packaging played an important role in promoting the sale of Britains figures. Attractive illustrated labels adorned the lids of the strawboard boxes—covered in a distinctive red paper—that were a trademark of the firm. Over the years, several artists were employed in designing these, but the

(continued on page 200)

Britains' Royal Naval landing parties (second and third versions) go into action while a Mignot warship covers them from offshore.
Burtt Ehrlich Collection   Height: 54 mm

Among the many types of Royal Navy sailors issued by Britains were these dapper fellows in straw hats.
Burtt Ehrlich Collection
                                                           Height: 54 mm

One of the rarest of all Britains toy soldier sets is the steel-helmeted version of a Royal Horse Artillery Gun Team at the gallop, which was produced for only a few years before World War II.

A rare Britains horse-drawn Royal Army Medical Corps ambulance with riders and orderlies in khaki service dress and steel helmets.
Burtt Ehrlich Collection
Height: Mounted figures: 70 mm

A column of British infantry in tropical dress (right), accompanied by Capetown Highlanders and King's African Rifles, marches across the sandy wastes of North Africa.
Burtt Ehrlich Collection   Height: 54 mm

By slight alterations of a basic figure and through paint variations,
Britains could use one model to represent several different units.
The two pictures on this spread show the following British
Commonwealth regiments: Union of South Africa Defense Force
and Durban Light Infantry.
Burtt Ehrlich Collection   Height: 54 mm

Among the rarer Britains sets is this one of the Regiment Louw
Wepener of South Africa. At a recent Phillips, New York, auction
sale, a set like the one pictured above sold for $2,600.
Burtt Ehrlich Collection   Height: 54 mm

The Second Dragoon Guards (Queen's Bays) with an original
Whisstock box.
Burtt Ehrlich Collection   Height: 70 mm

Britains added several new bands to its toy soldier lines in the
interwar years. At left we see a British military band in khaki service
dress; on the right, the Band of the Royal Marines in review order.
Burtt Ehrlich Collection   Height: 54 mm

A detachment of Grenadier Guards is inspected by a mounted officer.
Burtt Ehrlich Collection   Height: Mounted figure: 70 mm
                                                    Foot: 54 mm

A group of pre-World War II Irish Guards running at the trail.
Burtt Ehrlich Collection   Height: 54 mm

Now a rare set, this box of Britains infantry officers included officers from six different regiments, as well as a plume-bedecked field marshal.
Burtt Ehrlich Collection   Height: 54 mm

The Royal Marine Artillery, with the first version on the left and the second version on the right.
Burtt Ehrlich Collection   Height: 54 mm

In addition to units of the Regular Army, Britains also issued sets
representing soldiers of the Territorial Army, among them the
Middlesex Imperial Yeomanry.
Burtt Ehrlich Collection   Height: 70 mm

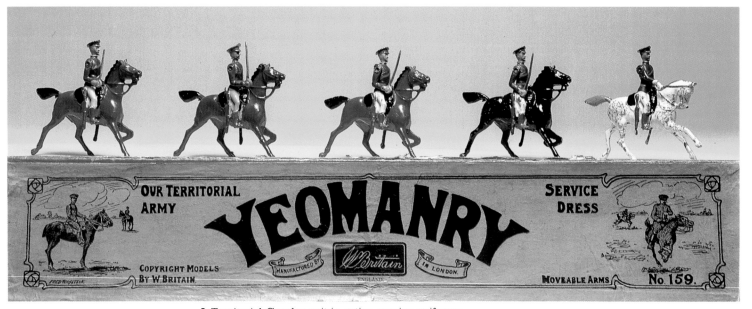

A Territorial Cavalry unit in active-service uniforms.
Burtt Ehrlich Collection   Height: 70 mm

An example of Britains' "Soldiers on Parade" series, produced briefly in the 1930s. A special baseboard into which the soldiers could be slotted permitted them to be displayed in formation.
Burtt Ehrlich Collection   Height: 54 mm

A rare set of Britains' Territorial Army with the soldiers in dress blue uniforms.
Burtt Ehrlich Collection   Height: 54 mm

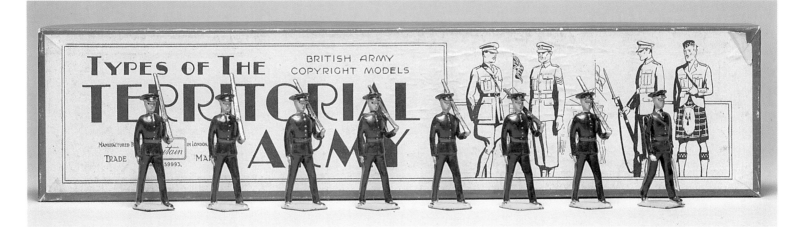

principal and most prolific of them was Fred Whisstock. Beginning in the years just before World War I and continuing until the early 1930s, Whisstock created individualized labels for each of the hundreds of British, colonial, and foreign units produced by Britains. Typical is the box lid for Set Number 120, the Coldstream Guards, showing the figures firing from the kneeling position; on the left is the regimental badge, the Star of the Order of the Garter, under which is the familiar signature of the illustrator; on the right a drawing of a Guardsman, shown as he would be found in the box—kneeling and firing; in the center, in bold letters, the words "British Soldiers, The Coldstream Guards," below which, on either side of the "W. Britain" trademark, are listed the regimental battle honors. In their own day, Whisstock boxes undoubtedly did much to entice youngsters browsing the counters of toyshops; today they are avidly sought by adult collectors.

The multitude of new military items and civilian lines brought out during the interwar years was more than the original factory—located at 24 Lambton Road in Hornsey Rise—could handle. Expansion was essential, and in the 1920s a second plant was constructed in the London suburb of Walthamstow. The new facility, dubbed the "North Light Building," had a skylight roof that provided a source of natural illumination for the women painters. Some 300 workers were now employed by the company. The eleven-hour workday began at 7:30 and ended at 6:30, and anyone who arrived more than three minutes after the morning whistle was docked half a day's pay. In a recent interview, Dennis Britain recalled how he and his father, William, Jr., would sit in the company boardroom each Friday afternoon stuffing pay envelopes. Wages ranged from 12 shillings and 6 pence weekly for an apprentice painter to 3 pounds for a top caster capable of producing 3,000 figures (roughly 20 gross) daily.

Despite long hours and strict work rules, Britains had no difficulty in keeping employees, most of whom spent their entire working lives with the firm. Pay scales were competitive with those of other industries and the company was known for its enlightened treatment of employees, who were recruited mainly from a small circle of families with long-standing ties to the firm. Actually, as Joanne and Ron Ruddell report in their short historical sketch of the company, *The Britains Collector's Checklist* (Vol. III), "it was impossible to get a job at Britains unless someone from the applicant's family was already employed there. Over the years, that became a tradition: fathers, sons, daughters, brothers and sisters all worked for the same company."

Although the Great Depression caused a temporary economic setback, necessitating price cuts, growth was steady in the 1930s. Britains even had to add a third factory as a result of a highly successful promotional gimmick to boost the sales of Cadbury's cocoa. Having started a Cococub Club for kids in the mid-thirties, the people at Cadbury discovered that many of the letters flowing into the club's newsletter contained requests for information about birds and animals. From this came the brainstorm to issue a series of Cadbury Cubs—humanized birds and animals—in specially marked cocoa tins. Britains was contracted to produce the little creatures, who bore such cute names as Mrs. Crackle*goose* or *Hen*rietta Fussyfeathers. Neither Cadbury nor Britains was quite prepared for the overwhelming response. Demand for Cococubs was so great that production schedules for other Britains figures were thrown into disarray. To deal with this, Britains hastily opened a factory at Colne in Lancashire whose only function was the production of Cadbury Cococubs.

By the end of the 1930s, with 500 workers now on the payroll, three factories going full blast, and more than 20,000,000 items being produced yearly, it could fairly be said that Britains was the world's leading manufacturer of toy soldiers, having far outstripped even the most prolific of its Continental rivals. Unfortunately, the zenith of the "Britains Empire" coincided with the rise of one being fashioned through terror and tyranny by Nazi Germany. Once again Europe was girding for war.

As the British Army improved its weaponry in anticipation of the coming conflict, the Britains army underwent a similar rearmament. A tentative movement toward

In the early 1930s, Britains added military and civilian aircraft to its
lines, beginning with a monoplane, which was offered in several
color variations. Illustrations are two post war color variations.
Burtt Ehrlich Collection

A detachment of the Carabinieri, Italy's famed paramilitary police. Before World War II, the set had eight men marching with rifles; after the war an officer figure (seen at both ends of the line) was added.
Burtt Ehrlich Collection   Height: 54 mm

As modern armies began to mechanize, the Britains army added motorized vehicles like this Carden-Lloyd tank, escorted by members of the Royal Tank Corps.
Burtt Ehrlich Collection   Height: 54 mm

A group of Britains staff cars both pre- and post-World War II, along with two Britains armored cars with swivel turrets. In the background are a Britains Nissen hut and an army barracks building produced briefly in the late 1930s. The marching figures are a rare set (No. 1834) Scots Guards in steel helmets.
Burtt Ehrlich Collection

ANTI-AIRCRAFT GUN

A really fine working model Anti-Aircraft Gun.

This model (firing a wooden shell) is manipulated in a manner similar to full-size machines. The barrel is elevated by quadrant and pinion gears, and traversing by pinion and internal toothed wheel. Loading and firing is semi-automatic, the operation being smooth yet positive.

COPYRIGHT MODELS   No. 1522
MANUFACTURED BY *W.Britain* IN LONDON, ENGLAND
TRADE   Regd. No. 459995   MARK

In anticipation of the Nazi blitz, Britains produced antiaircraft guns of various types.
Burtt Ehrlich Collection

Miniature barrage balloon units, scaled to accompany 00-gauge
model trains, provide protection against air attacks.
Burtt Ehrlich Collection

modernization began in the early 1930s with the appearance of a Carden–Lloyd tank (more of an armored personnel carrier by today's standards) and, soon after, a four-wheeled armored car with a swiveling gun turret. By the middle of the decade, mechanization was in full swing with motorized army lorries and tenders of various sizes, some wheeled, others with a combination of wheels and Caterpillar treads. Some were open, others were canvas-topped; always they came with hinged cab doors that opened and closed and back panels that flopped down. The monster of them all was an 18-wheeled affair, billed as an Underslung Heavy Duty Lorry, which was capable of carrying a large antiaircraft gun or a battery-operated searchlight.

To protect against air attack—an ominous prophecy of the blitz that was to come—Britains provided a full array of antiaircraft defense units and equipment. There were several different types of antiaircraft guns, one of which could be mounted on a mobile chassis; height finders, sound locators, and predictors, all with operators; spotters on swivel chairs; and a team of R.A.F. fire fighters in asbestos suits "so effective that these men can walk through flames without fear of danger." In smaller scale (corresponding to 00-gauge model trains), one could obtain a Miniature Barrage Balloon Unit, with winch lorry and balloon, along with an accompanying lorry and four-wheeled trailer piled high with hydrogen cylinders for use in inflating the barrage balloons.

Infantry now sallied forth in battle dress, with steel helmets and gas masks—charging, manning machine guns, digging entrenchments, throwing grenades, standing at the ready with bayoneted rifles and Tommy guns. Plenty of cannons were available, with steel-helmeted gunners to man them, and a Mobile Howitzer Unit to provide quick fire support for advancing infantry. To create a realistic setting for modern land warfare, Britains brought out, between 1939 and 1941, a series of army buildings. Included were a Nissen hut, guard room, gun shed, barracks buildings and parade ground setups, sandbagged emplacements for machine guns and artillery, pillboxes,

an open field shelter, and a Medical Corps casualty clearing station with a thatched-roof barn. Of short duration, these buildings, manufactured for Britains by another firm, are now highly valued for their rarity.

In marked contrast to the real Royal Air Force, which won the Battle of Britain, the Britains air force suffered from neglect and obsolescence. Just three antiquated aircraft were ready to take to the air in the event of an attack by enemy toy soldiers: a monoplane, a biplane, and a "Working Model of the 'Short' Monoplane Flying Boat with launching wheels." Two were single-engine airplanes and were unarmed—certainly no match for the Messerschmitt fighters and Junker bombers of the Luftwaffe. To this one could add a scale working model of a Direct-Control Autogiro (precursor of the modern helicopter), which could be made to glide through the air when attached—by means of a small wheel under the overhanging propeller—to a wire stretched across a room.

Surprisingly, the German armed forces received scant attention in the Britains catalogue—despite the fact that Germany was Great Britain's principal enemy in two major 20th-century wars. Early in its history, Britains had issued a set of spiked-helmeted Prussian infantry and another of colorful Prussian hussars. Around 1930, the firm added a lone set of modern German infantry in field-gray uniforms and coal-scuttle helmets. (Perhaps there was a subtle statement being made here about the restrictions on the size of the German Army imposed by the Versailles Treaty.) During the early years of World War II, Britains modestly augmented its "enemy" forces with Set Number 1895, "Pilots of the German Luftwaffe," a simple repainting of an earlier model of an R.A.F. pilot.

For two years after the outbreak of hostilities, Britains continued its production of toy models. But the impact of the war soon had its effect on the firm. "From the beginning of the War," states one of the firm's chroniclers, "the range and variety of figures started to decline and the general conditions and shortages of staff afterwards made necessary a severe contraction of the boxed lines. . . . The National Emergency on this occasion had more far-reach-

With the coming of World War II, Britains added timely items like this air raid warning post.
Burtt Ehrlich Collection
Height: 54 mm

A group of Britains military and civilian ambulances with both pre-World War II (square radiators) and postwar vehicles.
Burtt Ehrlich Collection

Listed in the catalogue as a "Working Model of the 'Short'
Monoplane Flying Boat," this aircraft is now extremely rare.
Burtt Ehrlich Collection

Britains' scale working model of a Direct Control Autogiro, precursor of the helicopter, could be had with either British or American markings.

Burtt Ehrlich Collection   Length: 21 cm

ing effects than in World War I, when there was continuous although limited production."

Many of Britains' employees were called to the colors, among them Dennis Britain, who went on active duty with the Royal Air Force. By 1942, the firm's three factories had retooled for defense work, turning out assorted parts for grenades, mines and other munitions. Britains did not emerge unscathed from the war. Although information is imprecise, one or more of its factories apparently were hit during German bombing attacks. More important, from a peak of success in 1939, the firm found itself six years later faced with the difficult task of rebuilding, almost from scratch, its distinguished lines of toy models.

Because it was produced for only one year, the Band of the Royal Marine Light Infantry, issued in 1938, is now the rarest of Britains bands. When a set belonging to actor Douglas Fairbanks, Jr., went on the auction block in 1977, it sold for nearly $1,400. In 1986, a set fetched $4,800 at auction.
Burtt Ehrlich Collection   Height: 54 mm

The U. S. Marine Corps Color Guard, issued briefly in the 1950s, seen here in its original box.
Burtt Ehrlich Collection

Height: 54 mm

Sunset of Empire

Britains quickly resumed toy production at war's end, bringing out a catalogue in the closing weeks of 1945. That first postwar catalogue, and those that followed during the next eight years, offered an extremely limited selection of some of the more popular prewar sets. As part of its effort to rebuild a war-ravaged economy, the British government, badly in need of foreign trade revenues, mandated that nonessential domestically manufactured goods be shipped abroad. The export-only policy meant that Britains models would not again be available in British shops until the early 1950s. It also accounts for the dramatic increase in toy soldier sets of foreign military forces.

The first of the Britains postwar international brigade was Belgium's Régiment des Grenadiers (Set No. 2009). In typical Britains fashion, this "new" figure was created by decapitating an earlier model of a French line infantryman of World War I and grafting on the head of a British fusilier. A similar bit of surgery just as easily transformed a British Guards officer in winter dress (from Set No. 312) into an officer for the Belgian regiment. Existing models were also used to create figures of the Soviet Union's Red Army Guards and Red Army Cavalry in parade uniform, and the Swedish Life Guard in ceremonial dress. Not all the new lines were cannibalized creations, however. Sets such as the Papal Swiss Guard and a Red Army infantry unit in summer uniform employed newly created figures, as did a later set of Denmark's Livgarde, the royal foot guards (although a companion set, the Danish Guard Hussar Regiment, was a reworking of the Prussian hussar model). The Danish foot guards were shown carrying their rifles in the distinctive cradle arms position familiar to all those who have seen them on guard duty at Copenhagen's Amalienborg Palace.

It was natural for Britains to further develop its already well-established American market. Particular emphasis was placed on producing United States military units, beginning with a set of marching U. S. Military Police, nicknamed "The Snowdrops" because of their white helmets, and followed by U. S. Army Air Corpsmen in 1949 pattern blue uniforms with slung carbines, and a 21-piece Band of the U. S. Marine Corps, "The President's Own," in full-dress scarlet tunics, blue trousers, and white caps. In the early 1950s, Britains brought out a series of American Civil War sets, capitalizing on a revival of interest in that conflict. Union and Confederate infantry sets featured soldiers in assorted action poses, and there were cavalrymen at the trot with carbines and artillery gun sets with cannon and gunners. The "Wild West" series was augmented by a Prairie Schooner (covered wagon), with a pioneer and his wife urging on a team of four galloping horses (also available in a larger display box with attacking Indians); a rodeo set with cowboys riding bucking broncos, lassoing steers, and fences to make corrals; and a two-tiered Wild West display of 90 pieces (Set No. 2061), with all manner of cowboys and Indians, steers, a corral, and assorted other props.

Additions were also made to the Latin American military line. In the early 1950s, the firm issued a series of Venezuelan soldiers, sailors, and military school cadets in single-row and display boxes, the largest of which featured a mix of marching sailors, cadets, and helmeted infantry with a standard-bearer. An earlier set of Uruguayan military school cadets, originally garbed in Napoleonic-style tall shakos and cutaway coats, was updated, with the cadets now wearing tunics and képis with a small plume.

Soon after the war, new British military models were brought out, beginning in the late 1940s with the appearance of airborne troops, the famed "Red Devils," in battle dress and red berets, and a most attractive figure of a ski trooper on skis in white snow uniform, which came both individually boxed and in a set of four. The coronation of Queen Elizabeth II in 1953 touched off a flurry of special sets and displays commemorating the ascension of the new monarch. First among these was a superb model of Queen Elizabeth herself, resplendent in the full-dress uniform of the Colonel-in-Chief of the Grenadier Guards, mounted sidesaddle—as she appeared at the annual Trooping the Colour ceremony. Completely new figures were fashioned for a box containing "The Royal Company of Archers, The Queen's Bodyguard for Scotland" (Set No. 2079); and there were displays of "The Sovereign's Standard and Escort" (Set No. 2067), with mounted trumpeters, farriers, and troopers of the Household Cavalry, and another of "The Household Cavalry Musical Ride" (Set No. 2085), featuring state trumpeters, a kettledrummer, and troopers of the Life Guards and Royal Horse Guards carrying lances.

The royal celebration of 1953 also prompted the release of what became known as the "Coronation" sets, a group of seven new issues depicting British units in "Number One Dress," a less showy type of ceremonial uniform adopted just before World War II. Available only from 1954 to 1959, the series (Set Nos. 2087–93) included a dismounted cavalry regiment, the Fifth Royal Inniskilling Dragoon Guards, several line-infantry regiments, among them the Gloucestershire Regiment, the Royal Irish Fusiliers, the Rifle Brigade, and the Parachute Regiment. The troops were either at attention, as they might have been while lining a processional route, or marching at the slope or at the trail. Adorning the sleeves of the Gloucestershires were two small light-blue armbands representing the American Presidential Unit Citation, awarded to the regiment for its service alongside United States troops in the Korean War. Completing this ceremonial series was a 25-piece Band of the Royal Berkshire Regiment. (From this point on, Britain's full bands would contain 25 pieces rather than 21.)

Britains, which had issued its own version of the well-known State Coach of England for the coronation of King George VI, now produced as a companion piece an excellent model of the State Open Road Landau. Seated in the open carriage were Queen Elizabeth and Prince Philip, with two attendants in a rear seat behind them. The landau was drawn by a team of six Windsor Grays, driven by three detachable outriders.

During this early 1950s renaissance, Britains brought out a group of medieval knights that are generally ranked among the finest toy soldiers produced by any firm. Issued under the heading "Knights of Agincourt" in 1954, the original figures had been created and cast several years earlier by master modeler Roy Selwyn-Smith. Under the auspices of Otto Gottstein, a distinguished collector of miniature soldiers and patron of the hobby, Selwyn-Smith set up a workshop near London's Ealing Common in January of 1951. In short order, he produced five mounted and five foot knights, all marvelously animated and no two exactly alike in stance. The figures, marketed under the trademark Selwyn Miniatures Ltd., were painted to the highest standard in accurate heraldic designs and were sold only in the United States.

"Unfortunately," Selwyn-Smith recalls, "the venture was short lived, in fact about nine months, and came to an end with the tragic death of Mr. Gottstein. The moulds were part of Mr. Gottstein's estate and had to be sold. I arranged that they should be offered to Britains Ltd., who after certain modifications put them on the market as 'Knights of Agincourt.'"

Although Britains had made great strides in rebuilding its toy soldier lines by the early 1950s—increasing the number of sets in its catalogue from a meager 103 in 1947 to nearly 400 in 1954—the postwar years presented a new set of production and cost problems. With demand for the firm's toys far outstripping its ability to supply them, new

Designed by Roy Selwyn-Smith, these mounted "Knights of
Agincourt" are among the finest toy soldiers produced by any
maker.
Burtt Ehrlich Collection   Height: 70 mm

A set of Algerian Spahis, produced briefly in the 1950s.
Burtt Ehrlich Collection   Height: 70 mm

In a scene reminiscent of *Beau Geste*, French Foreign Legionnaires, accompanied by mounted Spahis, march across the burning desert sands.
Burtt Ehrlich Collection
Height: Foot figures: 54 mm
Mounted: 70 mm

The Band of the Royal Scots Greys, the
last of the small group of mounted bands
issued by Britains.
Burtt Ehrlich Collection   Height: 70 mm

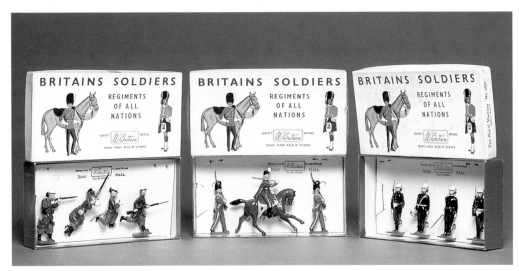

For a brief period in the late 1950s,
Britains produced what were called "half sets,"
which were less costly than normal-size sets.
Burtt Ehrlich Collection
              Height: Foot figures: 54 mm
                            Mounted: 70 mm

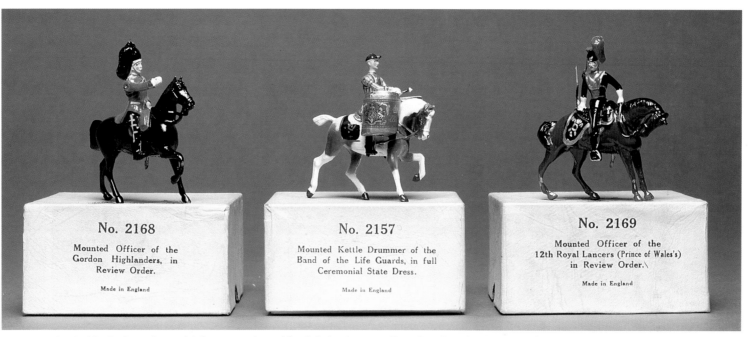

No. 2168
Mounted Officer of the
Gordon Highlanders, in
Review Order.

Made in England

No. 2157
Mounted Kettle Drummer of the
Band of the Life Guards, in full
Ceremonial State Dress.

Made in England

No. 2169
Mounted Officer of the
12th Royal Lancers (Prince of Wales's)
in Review Order.\

Made in England

A group of individually boxed special figures as issued by Britains in the 1950s.
Burtt Ehrlich Collection
Height: 70 mm

For a brief period in the 1950s, the U. S. Army Band was uniformed in bright yellow tunics. Britains issued a set showing the band in this distinctive but short-lived uniform. The set came without the goat.
Burtt Ehrlich Collection
Height: 54 mm

production methods had to be found. To increase its pool of painters, Britains resorted, for the first time in its history, to the use of outworkers, mainly women working at home. There are several versions of how this system originated, but according to a current Britains director, "Homework started just after the last war when a crippled girl living in the Archway area, not far from the factory in Hornsey, asked if she could paint models at home. The lead castings were put in surplus metal ammunition boxes, which was the way the models were transported around the factory, and four gross were delivered to her home. This method of painting proved successful, but it was still only supplementary to the hand painting in the factory."

A network of depots was set up where heavily laden vans brought cases of castings and paints. The women painters would pick up parcels of castings and paints at the beginning of the week and return the figures in finished form a few days later. When metal gave way to plastic in the 1960s, in-house painting was phased out. (Today all painting of Britains plastic figures is done by a force of 1,500 homeworkers, except for sample figures provided to them, and the unfinished models are packed in parcels of 100 instead of one gross.)

The postwar years also saw a burdensome increase in the cost of raw materials. Antimonial lead, the basic metal used, went from £40 per ton in 1938 to £200 per ton in the early 1950s. The price of the special paints, many of which were imported from Spain, shot up about 400 percent. A sympathetic article in the *New Statesman and Nation* (May 26, 1951) noted that "with much higher labour costs to be taken into account, there is no real case for grumbling from the nursery if the box of eight foot soldiers, which an unmonied uncle could provide for a florin [two shillings] ten years ago, now costs over eight shillings in the shops."

Britains made every effort to trim costs in order to keep price increases down to a minimum. With a few exceptions, the old illustrated labels were eliminated in favor of a standard box bearing the words "Britains Soldiers—Regiments of All Nations," with illustrations of a

Life Guard and Royal Scots Grey trooper at opposite ends of the lids of the cavalry boxes, and a Coldstream Guard and a Black Watch Highlander similarly positioned on the infantry box lids. Hoping to reach consumers with smaller purses, the firm introduced, in 1957, a limited selection of lower-priced "half boxes," containing either three or four figures. (These mini-sets lasted only until 1959). Smaller yet were the "picture packs." Dating from the late 1940s, they originally provided one or several farm and zoo series models in attractively illustrated, thin cardboard boxes. Military picture packs followed in 1954, and altogether there were some 125 individually packaged figures in this range, mainly of British and American military units and types.

A final change in the packaging of standard-size sets occurred in 1961, when the sturdy old strawboard boxes gave way to "window boxes" made of a cheaper cardboard. Although a cellophane panel in the top of the boxes permitted easy viewing of the figures inside, they lacked the charm and character of earlier types. (One English toy soldier dealer routinely refers to them in his lists as "cellophane-fronted monstrosities.") In a further effort to cut costs while maintaining quality, the number of figures in standard sets was reduced. After 1960, infantry sets had seven rather than eight figures, while cavalry boxes were cut from five to four pieces.

Despite these cost-saving measures, time was running out for metal toy soldiers. They simply could not effectively compete with cheaper plastics. With this in mind, Britains began to shift gears in the mid-1950s, purchasing a part interest in Herald Miniatures, the leading British manufacturer of plastic toy figures. In 1956, Britains completed the purchase of the Herald line, which was fully incorporated into the parent company's operations. With the acquisition of Herald, Britains also obtained the services of its master designer, Roy Selwyn-Smith—cited by John Garratt as "one of the most intelligent, capable and versatile makers of the models of the present century." From 1956 until the late 1960s, Selwyn-Smith designed most of the new models turned out by Britains. He was

Britains issued two versions of the U.S. Marine Corps Band,
"The President's Own." Above is the 25-piece summer dress version.
Burtt Ehrlich Collection   Height: 54 mm

also the creator of the "Swoppets," a series of plastic models with interchangeable headgear, weapons, and equipment, as well as heads and torsos that could be turned in different directions.

Ironically, the move into plastics came at a time when the firm had restored its metal lines almost to their prewar peak. In fact, the second half of the 1950s saw the issuance of many interesting new metal sets. Probably the most productive year was 1956, dubbed the "Collector's Year" by Britains. During that year the firm brought out a series of military bands (Set Nos. 2108–17), among them the Highland Pipe Band of the Black Watch; the U. S. Army Band in its short-lived yellow full-dress tunics; and another version of the U. S. Marine Band in summer uniform. Both of the latter were 25-piece bands, as was a Full Band of the Grenadier Guards, augmented with saxophones and French horns and featuring a unique drum major in state dress with a jockey-style cap. (As an indication of future trends, however, plastic drums were substituted for the old metal variety.)

For the export market, Britains brought out the Fort Henry Guards, a colorful Canadian unit in an 1860s uniform. A Fort Henry Guard fife and drum band, available in five- or ten-piece boxes, was subsequently added, and still later came two British line regiments—the 49th and 89th Foot—that had served at Fort Henry during the War of 1812, participating in the Battle of Chrysler's Farm. Most of these sets, and several figures sold individually as picture packs, were available only in Canada, at the Fort Henry gift shop.

Another part of the Americas was also favored with several export-only specials. Around 1959 a set of Bahamas Police and accompanying Bahamas Police Band went on sale in the popular tourist mecca. The black policemen were shown standing at attention in white jackets and sun helmets and contrasting dark-blue pants, and the set included a black sergeant and a British officer. The full band was the largest ever by Britains—26 pieces—and included a white bandmaster, a black drum major, a large

brass section (four trumpets, four trombones, two French horns, and a euphonium), saxophones, clarinets, fifes, and the usual drummers and cymbalist. (There was also a smaller version with 13 pieces.) Available only in one store in Nassau, the islands' principal town—and for only a short time—the Bahamas Police sets are among the rarest Britains. (A complete eight-piece box of the policemen, for example, recently sold at auction for $1,900.)

For Britains, 1959 was a watershed year. The firm began to prune down its line of metal models while expanding its production of plastic toys; these were made at a more spacious facility on Sutherland Road in Walthamstow, which, in the 1940s, had superseded the North Light Building. But even as the curtain descended on the age of the metal toy soldier, Britains managed a last hurrah. In that busy year of 1959, it brought out its last new metal model, a picture-pack figure of a bearded Fort Henry Guard Pioneer, both hands on the handle of an ax whose head rested on the ground. It was an exceptional figure, prompting L. W. Richards to remark that "If this was to be the last of the new metal figures by Britains, then it must be said that it was a 'Grandstand Finish.'"

The march into plastics was by now inexorable, spurred initially (and mainly) by cost factors and later by statutory regulations restricting the use of lead in toys. By 1960, only 142 metal sets remained in the catalogue. Two years later, lead models were being produced exclusively for export; and by the mid-1960s, metal models constituted only about one-tenth of Britains' total output. The sun finally set on the Britains empire of metal toy soldiers in 1966, the year the company stopped producing traditional lead figures. As Joe Wallis informs us in *Regiments of All Nations*: "By then the farm wagons were drawn by plastic horses; the metal artillery pieces were still produced, although of inferior metal; and the last two items of the old lines (the Landau and the Coronation Coach) were withdrawn after 1967. . . . An era of fine craftsmanship that had generated a superior line of toys had come to an end. *Sic transit gloria*."

The Bahamas Police Band, one of the rarest Britains sets, was sold
only in the Bahamas.
Burtt Ehrlich Collection   Height: 54 mm

Copycats and True Competitors

Britains enjoyed a domestic monopoly in the manufacture of toy soldiers during the first decade of its existence. But as the hollow-cast figure proved itself in the marketplace, other entrepreneurs jumped on the bandwagon. Around 1900 several firms sprouted in the London area. For the most part, only their names are worth recording, since their toy troops were distinguished mainly by a lack of originality and an obvious tendency to borrow freely from Britains' designs. In fact, the succession of lesser makers that emerged in the early 1900s might well be termed the parade of the pirates.

The earliest of these (between 1900 and 1905) were C. D. Abel, Hanks Brothers, Davies & Company, David Mudie, and James Renvoize. They were followed, from 1910 to 1914, by Russell Manufacturing and A. Fry. Their product lines, so far as they are known, closely duplicated such Britains basics as guardsmen and line infantrymen in marching or running positions, Highlanders, British sailors, and khaki-clad infantry in various poses. A few, like Renvoize and Abel, made Russian and Japanese troops of the 1904–5 war; while Fry focused on World War I soldiers from some of the nations engaged in that conflict. Boy Scouts, North American Indians, and Zulus were popular themes, and the Boer War also served as an inspiration for the first of the copycat companies. Both James Renvoize and Hanks Brothers issued pirated versions of Britains' "Imperial Yeomanry," which proved to be their undoing.

Dismayed by such flagrant acts of piracy, William Britain and his clan struck back with a series of lawsuits. In 1901, Hanks and Renvoize were hauled before the King's Bench, a division of the High Court of Justice, where Britains requested and was granted "an injunction restraining the Defendants, their servants and agents, and each and every of them, from infringing the Plaintiff's copyright dated 1st June, and known as the 'Imperial Yeoman.'" In 1902, two other pirates, Davies & Company and David Mudie, were also made to walk the judicial plank for having reproduced Britains' metal busts of King Edward VII and his queen. In every instance, the High Court's decision required the errant firm to hand over or destroy all copies and molds of the pirated models, and also authorized Britains to recover court costs and damages. These decisions, which helped to stem the pirate plague, were reprinted in Britains catalogues with a cautionary note that legal proceedings would quickly be taken against anyone "manufacturing, selling or otherwise disposing of any pirated copies of W. Britain & Sons' Copyright Models of Soldiers, Horses, Statuary, etc." For years afterward, Britains remained wary, and catalogues well into the 1930s carried the warning: "When buying Britains soldiers see that they are Britains."

Not all of the early hollow-cast competitors were pirates. BMC, which started operations sometime before 1914, brought out quality figures of its own design, although like the others it often played follow-the-leader in its choice of subjects. Like Britains, it featured the cavalry and infantry regiments of the British Regular Army, to which were added troops of the major combatants of the Great War and a few civilian types—among them Boy Scouts, Girl Guides, and fire fighters. More imaginatively posed than Britains', BMC's action figures are truly that: a mounted Cossack strains forward in the saddle, sword raised high overhead, ready to deliver a vicious swipe at a foeman; a member of the Rifle Brigade goes into action, legs stretched apart, one foot slightly higher than the other, as if climbing a hill; a French *poilu* advances with the purposeful look of a man determined to plant the Tricolor on the enemy breastworks. BMC figures came with both fixed and movable arms.

Around 1910, C. W. Baker began marketing toy soldiers under the trademark Reka (with bases sometimes marked "Reka, Copyright C. W. Baker"). Quality varied and many models were patterned after Britains, but the range included such variations as bandsmen standing at attention (rather than marching), Italian Bersaglieri with detachable entrenching tools, and mounted troops with removable riders. Reka appears to have actively courted the American market; its substantial line of United States troops came in a far greater assortment of poses than Britains and included such interesting sets as a U. S. Army Horse Artillery gun team and a U. S. Army medical service unit.

The most notable exception to the pirate band was the firm of John Hill & Company, more popularly known as Johillco, which was founded around 1900 by a former Britains employee. A worthy competitor of Britains, Johillco rapidly rose to the number-two slot among hollow-cast makers, its range of offerings and productivity rivaling that of Britains. Emphasis was on individual figures rather than boxed sets, which in the military line numbered fewer than 200. No effort was made to mimic Britains' thorough coverage of British military and naval units, or its constantly expanding list of foreign troops. And although occasionally topical, Johillco was content to stay primarily with catalogue basics: troops in full dress and battle gear, and farm, zoo, railroad, and hunting figures.

If there was one major deficiency in Johillco's models, it was inconsistency in design. It has been said that Johillco made some of the best and some of the worst toy soldiers; and if one were to do a detailed survey of the firm's figures, one could borrow the title of a popular motion picture and call them "the good, the bad, and the ugly." Some of the best models are to be found in Johillco's various civilian ranges. Here we have such imaginative pieces as a blacksmith shoeing a horse, a running British

policeman blowing his whistle and brandishing a billy club, and another standing feet apart, flashing his night lantern (available both in 54 mm and 68 mm), conveying perfectly in his demeanor the pride and self-confidence of the prototypical British bobby. Cowboys come on bucking broncos, twirling lassos or firing rifles over lying horses; and there are such unusual types as a tramp carrying his meager possessions in a bundle on a stick, an innkeeper in white apron, and a bride and groom taking the vows before a village parson.

Johillco's railroad and farm figures are more varied than Britains'. A large railroad display set boasts not only the usual station staff and porters with hand trolleys, but an array of accessories including ticket- and candy-dispensing machines, a scale (or "weighing machine" as it is called in the catalogue), a lamppost, and a station signboard. Passengers, too, show more individuality; there is an elderly man with a cane, a bowler-hatted gentleman with a coat draped over his arm, and a dapper young chap with a straw boater. The ladies are equally varied and are found carrying bags, sitting reading books, or walking with the ever-present and so-necessary umbrella. The "Miniature Farmyard" had such accessories as a windmill, rabbit hutch, chicken coop, pigsty, forge (for the various blacksmiths), well with bucket, and even a young woman in a punt—a popular pole-propelled boat used for river outings.

As earlier noted, Johillco's military sets were mainly undistinguished, with, in most cases, no officer or musician to break up the monotony of rows of marching, charging, or firing troops. Military models vary greatly in style, an indication that several modelers of differing abilities were employed. Some extremely poor types include the kneeling and prone Highlanders in tropical dress and the charging infantryman in khaki service dress; and there seems to have been no great effort to keep mounted men proportionally in scale with foot figures. Horsemen also have a thin, almost emaciated look by comparison to their heftier companions on foot.

Johillco made much less use of the movable-arm

Britains' chief competitor was the firm of John Hill & Company, better known as Johillco. Although most of their figures were made in the standard 54mm scale, they also produced smaller-scale figures such as this coronation display set.

Burtt Ehrlich Collection

Height: Foot figures: 30 mm
Mounted: 45 mm

The ornate box lid from Johillco's coronation display set.
Burtt Ehrlich Collection

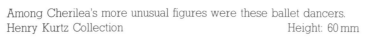

Among Cherilea's more unusual figures were these ballet dancers.
Henry Kurtz Collection   Height: 60 mm

During the Russo-Finnish War
(1939–40), Johillco brought out this
Finnish ski trooper.
Henry Kurtz Collection
                                    Height: 54 mm

feature that was so much a part of Britains, and consequently had more freedom in posturing its figures. (As one authority remarked, "There is not much you can do with a movable-arm infantryman except make him march at the slope or trail.") Where Britains' toy troops are straight-backed, disciplined fellows marching in their flawless ranks, Johillco's toy soldiers have distinctive personalities. A mounted Scots Greys trumpeter reins in his horse and sounds a call; a nurse kneels to comfort a wounded man; a Finnish ski trooper in heavy winter coat and hood advances with the stolidity and determination that characterized the Finns' gallant defense of their homeland against Soviet Russian invaders during the 1939–40 Winter War.

Because Johillcos were sold individually, they were more accessible. According to Shamus Wade, an English toy soldier dealer, Johillcos are more likely to be found in the homes of blue-collar families, while Britains prevail in higher-income households—and not simply because they cost less. "Could it be," asks Wade, "because Johillco Other Ranks [enlisted men] are individuals . . . while Britains Other Ranks are obedient, anonymous and identical figures ordered about (in step) at the behest of their betters?"

Johillco had no consistent pattern of producing historical figures, but it did turn back the clock to ancient times, issuing a richly detailed Roman chariot with two-horse team and charioteer, and a "Roman Arena" set with gladiators, chariots, and several large, overbearing tigers. As part of its later effort to exploit the American market, soldiers of the American Civil War were turned out; but these, unfortunately, would have to be listed among the bad and the ugly. On the other hand, the good was very much represented by Ethiopian troops, particularly an outstanding mule-borne mountain battery and a realistic stretcher team, brought out at the time of the Italian invasion of 1935. The Russo–Japanese War and World War I resulted in a scattering of foreign units, but these rarely lasted more than a few years after the particular conflict. Johillco's only real overseas interest was the United States,

which was served up a selection of soldiers in battle dress, U. S. Marines, West Point cadets, and two National Guard units, the 7th New York and 71st New York State Militia regiments.

One British unit that caught the fancy of Johillco and several of the other hollow-cast makers was the London Scottish, a unit of the Territorial Army (comparable to the National Guard in the United States). In the early days of World War I, the London Scottish, in their eye-catching hodden-gray kilts and blue glengarries, earned the distinction of being the first Territorial unit to reach France and the first to see action. At Messines, on October 31, 1914, the regiment gallantly assaulted the German positions, sustaining nearly 400 casualties. Both Britains and Fry commemorated the event with charging models of the London Scottish; while BMC issued its version marching at the slope. The Johillco figure showed the gray-clad Highlanders kneeling and firing.

Johillco produced a creditable series of civilian motor vehicles—far more extensive than the Britains "Motor Road" series. Included were mail and delivery vans, sedans and coupés, motor coaches and lorries. There was also a fire engine equipped with a winch-operated ladder and manned by six fire fighters. Among the firm's novelty items were a batch of water pistols and a squirting camera. Johillco's various markings, found under the base or on the figure itself, were "John Hill," "J. Hillco," "Jo Hill," and "Johillco." When the firm began producing plastic figures in the 1950s, the trademark became "Hilco, Made in England."

Only two of the early hollow-cast competitors of Britains survived beyond the difficult years of World War I. Reka continued its operations until the early 1930s, when it sold off its molds and closed its doors. Johillco maintained its position as the second largest British toy soldier maker throughout the interwar years. However, the firm suffered a severe setback during World War II, when its London factory was destroyed by German bombs; and although new facilities were built after the war, Johillco

Between the two world wars, several new hollow-cast toy soldier makers began operations. Among them was the firm of Crescent, which produced this set of knights and crusaders.
Henry Kurtz Collection   Height: Foot figures: 54 mm
                                                      Mounted: 65 mm

never completely regained its earlier standing. Nor did the switch to plastic in the 1950s provide salvation for the firm, which ended production in the 1960s.

The interwar years witnessed the emergence of three new toy soldier companies: Charbens & Company, Crescent Toy Company, and Taylor and Barrett. The last of these was also the least in its impact, producing a modest range of standard-size hollow-casts, including some interesting nonmilitary models, and eventually splitting into Taylor and Sons Cast Metals and Barrett and Sons. Like Johillco, Charbens and Crescent focused on individual pieces rather than boxed sets. Both issued a predictable blend of old standbys: Guardsmen, Highlanders, Household Cavalry, and modern military types in battle dress.

Charbens, founded in 1930, produced hollow-casts in 54-millimeter and sometimes smaller sizes, along with an unbreakable die-cast metal range. Among the more interesting items found in its catalogues are a large display set of the British Eighth Army, with 18 soldiers and an armored car, and a companion set of the Afrika Korps with a similar composition. Then, too, there were pirates and paratroopers, Foreign Legionnaires and frogmen, lots of knights mounted and on foot, a nice group of circus figures, and, later, a series of American GIs. Probably the most interesting toys by Charbens were its horse-drawn and motorized vehicles. Among these were a charming baker's van with horse and delivery man; a fire engine set featuring a truck with ladder that could be raised and lowered; and a travelling zoo set containing two wheeled cages bearing assorted animals and hauled by an elephant.

Crescent entered the toy business in 1922 but apparently did not turn out toy solders until 1930. Its figures were mainly fixed arm and 54 millimeter, and the quality ranged from poor to acceptable. Initially, the firm may have purchased molds from Reka, and some figures appear to be remakes of Fry models. Some exotic and unusual figures appeared, among them a Maori tribesman doing a war dance, and an 18th-century highwayman with

pistol, curiously listed in the catalogue under "Medieval Models." Boxed sets were largely put together from existing individual models, leading at times to odd assortments. In later years, boxes with attractive four-color lid illustrations replaced earlier unadorned red-and-yellow boxes.

Following in the Britains tradition, Crescent issued a Royal Horse Artillery gun team and a British naval brigade that parroted the Britains naval landing party. Most interesting were its smaller boxed sets, such as a Royal Engineers unit stringing a telephone line, a "Searchlight" unit with two-man crew, and a deep-sea diver with detachable helmet and separately cast tools that fit into a small ring replacing the diver's right hand. Export to the United States led to some interesting issues, among which was a New York City Police set that contained a mounted policeman with detachable rider, and officers on foot in winter and summer uniforms. The company also produced small-scale ships and planes, and miniature garages and service stations.

After World War II, there was another small explosion of toy soldier makers, and as Ian McKenzie reports, "Names like Stoddart Ltd., Benbros, Roydon, Sacul and Astra-Pharos . . . each left a small contribution to enrich the records." Most of these newcomers, like shooting stars, appeared and disappeared fairly quickly. Two exceptions that did more than merely dent the market were Timpo and Cherilea Products. Starting in 1948, Cherilea turned out a full range of British ceremonial troops and American and British khaki-clad combat soldiers of decent but not exceptional quality. Medieval knights were plentiful and included, as part of the "Baronial Series," a superior model of the Black Prince and another of a 15th-century knight in Gothic armor and tournament trappings. Both riders were detachable from their mounts and the Knight came with removable accessories—sword, shield, battle-ax, and helmet. It is believed that these figures were the work of Wilfred Cherrington, an associate of Richard Courtenay, whose masterful

Founded in 1948, the firm of Cherilea produced a line of toy soldiers
that included the usual British Guardsmen, seen here stitched to a
fort backing strip.
Henry Kurtz Collection
Height: Foot figures: 54 mm
Mounted: 70 mm

For the American market, Cherilea brought out a set of American baseball players.
Burtt Ehrlich Collection   Height: 54 mm

medieval knights are well known to collectors of model soldiers.

Among Cherilea's more unusual and interesting figures were a group of ballet dancers in various poses. The three ballerinas and their male dancer companion are nicely proportioned and slightly larger than standard size. A popular "Spacemen Series" featured, in addition to an assortment of ray-gun-toting space soldiers (complete with removable oxygen masks), rocket ships and launch pads, as well as such exotic extraterrestrials as an Ant Man and a Giant Worm. Cherilea was taken over by another firm in 1973, by which time it had made the transition to plastic models. Some of these are still being issued under another trademark.

By far the most significant of the postwar makers was Timpo, which actually started up during the final years of the war. Timpo (an acronym for Toy Importers) stressed action and activity in its miniatures, which in design often rivaled the best of Britains and other leading toy soldier producers. "Remove the sentiment attached to Britains," states John Garratt, "and Timpo emerges as probably the most consistently good of the later manufacturers." A look through one of the firm's 1950s catalogues reveals a strong emphasis on civilian models—farm, zoo, circus, and police—and, if one excludes combative cowboys and Indians, only 13 of 45 pages are given over to military figures. Unlike most of its domestic competitors, Timpo did not devote much effort to British military units, which merit only a scant three pages in the catalogue. By contrast, there are six pages of United States soldiers and sailors, four of West Point cadets, and 11 more of Wild West figures—an understandable emphasis, since export to the United States accounted for the bulk of Timpo's sales.

Timpo's World War II GIs are often cited as the best toy models of modern U. S. combat troops by a non-American maker. Designed by Roy Selwyn-Smith, who was responsible for many of Timpo's finest models, they project the casual toughness of the American citizen-soldier.

Here we have no idealized notions of troops in battle, with every tunic button in place. Instead, as the GI Joes struggle forward under fire, sometimes crouching or crawling, they have the businesslike air of soldiers who do not care much for uniforms or war. Helmets tilted back, baggy trousers tucked into combat boots, they fire Tommy guns, rifles, and bazookas, hurl grenades, sweep the ground with mine detectors, or man mortars. Back in camp, they lounge about with rolled-up sleeves, washing clothes or eating. Available as individual pieces, they could also be obtained in small boxes of 6 or 7 figures or larger displays with as many as 24 different types. An innovation was their presentation—under the heading "U. S. Army Camp Units"—in minidioramas, such as a mortar team with mortar and sections of barbed wire, and a field headquarters with a small hutch. In each of these, the figures were sewn straight up on a cardboard platform, which was then inserted into special boxes four to six inches deep.

Less satisfactory are Timpo's West Point cadets. Although the postures are considerably more varied than those of other hollow-cast makers, the company's research was not up to par. Timpo's West Pointers are incorrectly garbed in uniforms similar to those worn by cadets at another American military school, the Citadel in South Carolina. The firm's cowboys and Indians are a well-animated and colorful lot, with such clever originals as two cowboys sitting around a campfire playing guitar and accordion. A Conestoga wagon came with a real canvas top. There was also a "Hopalong Cassidy" series, based on the adventures of the popular Western film star, that featured Hopalong and his sidekicks Lucky and California. Comic strips served as inspiration for models of Captain Marvel, Captain Midnight, Tarzan, and Superman.

Just as some toy soldier companies followed the flag, Timpo followed the films. Beginning in the early 1950s, with the issuance of figures from the motion picture version of *Ivanhoe*, the firm produced a much-admired series of medieval models based on characters in historical films then being turned out by Hollywood. Somewhat heftier and slightly taller than standard Timpo figures (which generally were 56 mm), the "Ivanhoe" series featured knights on foot and mounted on sturdy chargers. Like all of Timpo's equestrian models, the riders were detachable from their horses. Some helmets had movable visors and tufts of furry material to simulate a plume.

The success of the "Ivanhoe" figures led to another medieval group, this one depicting King Arthur and his Knights of the Round Table. Most notable here was the figure of King Arthur, sword arm upraised, resplendent in crown and robe. The last of the motion pictures sets was the "Quentin Durward" series. Inspired by the 1955 Metro-Goldwyn-Mayer Cinemascope epic, it included figures of Quentin Durward and other principals, as well as royal guardsmen and Landsknechts bearing swords, crossbows, lances, and pikes. Weapons were cast separately and therefore were interchangeable. Originally, the lances were made of metal, but later, because of breakage problems, plastic was used. The "Quentin Durward" series marked the end of Timpo's new metal models. Beginning in 1956, metal figures were phased out in favor of plastic remakes.

Timpo was one of a small group of British hollow-cast makers that successfully made the transition to plastic. Among those that survived the switch, Britains remains preeminent. Today the firm turns out more than 16,000,000 models annually, making it, as in its earlier metal heyday, the world's leading manufacturer of toy soldiers. Its latest catalogue leans heavily toward civilian themes, with more than half the pages given over to farm and wildlife models—including an array of trucks and tractors and such modern improvements as mechanized combine harvesters and helicopter crop sprayers. Military miniatures and other combatants are limited to a few pages of cowboys, Indians, and 7th Cavalrymen; soldiers of the American Civil War; a series of medieval knights; and British, German, and American troops and vehicles of the World War II period.

Keeping up with modern trends, the firm produces a space series, complete with spaceships, space soldiers, and alien intruders, and a host of accessories useful in waging interplanetary warfare on playroom floors. Under "Metal Models," some thirty boxed sets and individual items are currently listed. They include a predictable mix of Foot Guards, Household Cavalrymen, Highlanders, and such tourist favorites as London Bobbies, Beefeaters, and Queen Elizabeth uniformed and mounted for Trooping the Colour. With the American market in mind, the company now issues several boxed sets of U. S. Marines in dress blues. All come packaged in cellophane-fronted "window boxes" and are made of a lightweight metal alloy. Certainly it is a far cry from the golden age of metal. Nevertheless, collectors may still be thankful that a venerable name is being kept alive and that a glorious tradition of quality toy making is being maintained.

Of the half-dozen hollow-cast firms that started up after World War II, the most significant was Timpo. Its well-designed range of figures included this boxed "Big Game Hunting" set.
Burtt Ehrlich Collection

Considered by many the finest toy soldier representations of
American GIs, these Timpo action figures were designed by Roy
Selwyn-Smith.
Ernest Schwartz Collection   Height: 54 mm

A detail shot of a Timpo GI with a mine detector.
Ernest Schwartz Collection   Height: 54 mm

CHAPTER IV
THE AMERICAN MAKERS
The Dime-Store Doughboys

The United States was a latecomer among the major producers of metal toy soldiers, relying almost exclusively on European imports until the early years of the 20th century. Some German flats certainly made their way into the American colonies in the 18th century; in 1760, for example, a London dealer shipped a quantity of toys, including a set of Prussian dragoons, to a Virginia gentleman named George Washington. The dragoons, presumably German-made tin flats, were intended for Washington's stepson John Parke Custis and cost the future American president 1 shilling and 3 pence.

Nearly twenty years later, in 1777, as General Washington and his ragged Continental Army struggled through the winter of their discontent at Valley Forge, New York City residents thumbing through the December 1777 issue of the *Royal Gazette* would have come across an advertisement for toy soldiers. Under the heading "Christmas Presents for the Young Folks," the miniature figures were described as being "cast in metal, in beautiful uniforms," and were priced at 18 shillings per dozen. No specifics about place of manufacture were given, but in all likelihood they came from Nuremberg or one of the other German cities where production of tin soldiers had recently commenced on a large scale. Perhaps, as one authority suggests, they were brought to the American colonies on the same ships that carried the thousands of German mercenaries who formed the bulk of the British forces serving in the American Revolutionary War.

Little more can be said about toy soldiers in the early years of the American republic except to note that if any domestic manufacturers did exist, they were obviously of short duration and little consequence. A few nonmilitary flats dating from the early 1800s have come to light, but whether they were made in the United States or brought over from Germany is unclear. Some faltering efforts at domestic production seem to have been made in the 1850s; surviving specimens include flat figures, unpainted and engraved on only one side, of a cavalryman mounted with sword in hand, and an infantryman in a militia-type shako and frock coat standing stiffly at attention. Both figures are crudely designed, the infantryman being especially primitive. The cavalryman is slightly more realistic—although the rider is far too large for his horse—and wears the Hardee-style hat and shoulder scales of a regular U. S. Cavalryman of the period.

A more elegant looking and accurately scaled group of tin figures representing American Civil War Zouaves was recently put on display at the West Point Museum. Whether or not these large-size flats are American made cannot be stated with certainty, but they seem to have been based on a wood engraving depicting the 5th New York Volunteer Infantry Regiment, better known as Duryée's Zouaves, which was published by a New York City printer in 1861. So similar in pose and uniform are the tin Zouaves to those shown in the print, that it may be fairly surmised that some enterprising local toy manufacturer, inspired by the illustration, decided to issue a miniature reproduction of the regiment.

The first significant manufacturer of toy soldiers in the United States was the firm of McLoughlin Brothers. Founded in 1854 by John McLoughlin, who took over a company that had been publishing children's books and

← Beginning in the mid-1930s, Brooklyn-born John Warren, Jr., produced a line of toy soldiers depicting United States troops of that period. A platoon of U. S. infantrymen snaps to attention as the colors are marched to the front.
Burtt Ehrlich Collection   Height: 60 mm

A group of large flat toy soldiers dating from the American Civil War period and possibly manufactured in the United States. The large infantry figures probably represent the 5th New York Duryee's Zouaves, a famous Civil War Regiment.
West Point Museum Exhibit   *Photo by Henry Kurtz*

One of the earliest American manufacturers of metal toy troops was the American Soldier Company, which produced a line of figures of late-19th-century American military types based on Britains models.
Henry Kurtz Collection   Height: 54 mm

Often thought to be American Soldier Company figures, these rather crude-looking hollow-cast U.S. infantrymen of the Spanish-American War are actually by the firm of McLoughlin Brothers.
Henry Kurtz Collection   Height: 55 mm

paper toys since 1828, the firm officially became known as McLoughlin Brothers of New York when Edmund McLoughlin formed a partnership with brother John in 1857. That same year, the company issued its first paper soldiers, a series of 4½- by 7-inch strips, each containing four or five figures of gaily uniformed American militiamen. This modest beginning was quickly followed by more elaborate displays, as an 1858 advertising blurb indicates: "Paper Soldiers for Boys. Two kinds: Soldiers on foot containing 28 pieces—soldiers on horse containing 18 pieces."

Paper soldiers had been popular playthings in Europe for more than a century, with some being produced as far back as the 1600s. As relatively cheap methods of color printing were developed in the 19th century, this particular variation of the traditional toy soldier became more widespread, achieving a high standard in both artistic quality and realistic coloring in the sheets issued by such notable companies as Pellerin and Rudolf Silbermann. Paper soldiers were inexpensive, costing only pennies, and easy to assemble. A youngster had only to carefully cut out the figure and paste it onto whatever cardboard scraps he could scrounge. Usually the cardboard-backed troops were affixed to pieces of wood or some other material so they would stand upright. Lined up in neat rows on their stands, they made inviting targets for pop-guns, peashooters, and spring-operated cannons.

Given their appeal to the creative as well as the aggressive instincts of the young, paper soldiers quickly caught on in the United States as they previously had in Europe. For generations of American boys and girls, from the 1850s to the end of World War I, McLoughlin Brothers was synonymous with paper soldiers. Constantly improving and refining its product, McLoughlin had, by the 1870s, expanded its range to include soldiers of the American Revolution, Highlanders, and Zouaves. Also available were cavalrymen "mounted on spirited horses, moving in every style of action from a sober trot to a wild gallop." The width of the strips now stood at 14½ inches

and the height of the individual figure was just over 4 inches. By the 1880s, the figures had grown to 5 inches and the number of types had been greatly enlarged, as James T. Lane informs us in the following description:

There were U. S. soldiers in brass-spiked helmets, dark blue jackets, and light blue pants; West Point Cadets in summer full dress uniforms; and smart Annapolis midshipmen. Quaintly bewhiskered U. S. sailors vied with stout Continentals and colorful U. S. Zouaves. Foreign troops were also on hand in goodly numbers. French soldiers in kepis and the old red-and-blue uniforms; Prussians in spiked helmets; British grenadiers in tall bearskins; and Highlanders in feather bonnets and kilts were all available. And there was no lack of martial music in McLoughlins' "Parade of the Paper Soldiers." Three different brass bands and a drum and fife corps were on hand to play the airs.

Later McLoughlin's paper troops were issued on square sheets 10¼ by 10¼ inches; and by the time World War I broke out, the company was also producing heavier cardboard figures, already cut out and attached to wooden-block stands. These could be purchased in boxed sets that contained as few as 5 or as many as 80 to 100 figures. The largest known display set was entitled "100 Soldiers on Parade" and came in an oversized presentation box that measured 12½ by 21½ inches.

Toward the end of the 19th century, probably in the 1890s, McLoughlin began producing solid-cast metal soldiers, becoming, as far as is known, the first major American maker to do so. Production seems to have been fairly extensive, with a wide range of types being offered through major toy retail outlets. Unfortunately, not many of the early McLoughlin metal models survived the ravages of time and childhood war games. Those that have indicate that the American company's figures were either outright piracies of Heyde designs or were made from

Among the U.S. toy soldier firms that used imported Britains models was the Eureka Metal Company of Brooklyn, New York, which, like Britains and the American Soldier Company, employed a special display tray designed by C. W. Beiser. The set illustrated contains American made figures.

Michael McAfee Collection

Photo by Michael McAfee

In the 1920s, the St. Louis
Soldier Company turned out
figures like these two American
militiamen, which were mainly
reworked Heyde and Britains
designs.
Steve Balkin Collection
Height: 54 mm

This clumsy-looking toy infantryman
by Ideal represents an early effort by
an American company to produce
a distinctly American line of toy soldiers.
Steve Balkin Collection   Height: 54 mm

Dime-store figures were America's unique contribution to the world
of the toy soldier. Simple and functional, they stood a head taller
than their European counterparts and were usually 80 mm in size.
Above, Barclay army and navy flag-bearers flank a third by their
chief competitor, Manoil.
Larry Levine Collection   Height: 80 mm

molds purchased from one of the German makers.

Not long ago, an interesting example of the McLoughlin solid-cast line was sold at auction in New York. Representing a U.S. National Guard infantry unit, this complete set consisted of 14 marching soldiers with rifles at the slope, a drummer, a flag-bearer, and mounted and foot officers—essentially the same composition as a standard Heyde infantry set. The figures themselves were strikingly similar in both appearance and size (roughly 50 mm) to small-scale Heydes. In packaging, too, McLoughlin borrowed a page from its European competitors and the set came in a sturdy box bearing an illustrated label reminiscent of those adorning Britains box lids. No manufacturer's trademark appears on these or other McLoughlin metal figures, but a peculiarity is the presence of two small depressions on the underside of the bases where the feet are plugged in. Michael McAfee of the West Point Museum suggests that the indentations may be the result of the mold being affixed to a pegged board "or something which projected up to hold it in place, yet also left two marks when the lead reached the bottom of the mold."

A possible insight into the McLoughlin line is to be found in an 1897 catalogue from F.A.O. Schwarz, the well-known New York City toy store. Among the offerings that year were "pewter soldiers," available in sets costing as little as 25 cents for a small box or as much as $10—a hefty sum for that day—for a large display. Sets were listed under such headings as "Parades," "Battles," "Naval Reviews," "Camps," and "Coast Defenses," while others covered civilian themes. Nothing is said about the manufacturer, which, judging from the catalogue illustrations, could be either McLoughlin or Heyde. But we have a clue as to origin in the catalogue's statement that "many styles are especially made for us, among them New York Militia," including the 7th, 22nd, and 69th regiments. It seems probable that Schwarz would have turned to a local firm like McLoughlin Brothers for such special issues, as opposed to the costlier alternative of having them made overseas. On the other hand, it could be argued just as easily that the extensive range of sets offered in the Schwarz catalogue, including zoos, hunting scenes, and other large displays, make it more likely the figures are Heydes, since McLoughlin is not known to have been so prolific in its output.

In the early 1900s, McLoughlin added 54 mm hollow-cast figures to its line of metal soldiers. Chunky in appearance, with oversized chests and proportionally short legs, they are not particularly eye-catching. Marching soldiers, in either the blue service dress or khaki campaign outfits of the Spanish-American War period, are rather static. Figures were cast in one piece, with rifles and other equipment molded on, and were on oval bases. A distinctive earmark of the McLoughlin hollow-cast is the large air hole on the left side of the head. Although coarse and unimaginative, these figures are nonetheless of interest to collectors as precursors of the more distinctive and successful dime-store figures that flooded the American market in the years between the two world wars.

McLoughlin Brothers faded away after World War I. In 1920, the company relocated from New York to Springfield, Massachusetts, where, as one commentator notes, "it disappeared in a cloud of uncertainty." It is believed that surviving members of the McLoughlin family may have sold out to the Milton Bradley Company, a major toy and game manufacturer, bringing to an end a sixty-three-year parade of paper and metal soldiers—the longest run by an American toy soldier maker.

Even murkier are the histories of several other American toy soldier manufacturers who came and went between the 1890s and the early 1920s. The American Soldier Company, based in Brooklyn, New York, began producing hollow-cast and solid-cast figures around the turn of the century. Over the years, collectors have noted that early models closely resemble figures produced by Britains during the first decade of its production. One American Soldier Company set featured an exact replica of Britains' first-version Somerset Light Infantryman stand-

All of the dime-store companies focused on troops in action. In the
battle scene here, we see the varied types produced by Barclay
and Manoil, the principal dime-store companies.
Larry Levine Collection   Height: 80 mm

Stretcher-bearers carry a wounded man to a field hospital while
nurses and doctors attend other casualties in this grouping of Barclay
figures.
Larry Levine Collection   Height: 80 mm

A Barclay signalman wigwags a message as his comrades man a
field telephone and a radio at a Signal Corps station.
Larry Levine Collection   Height: 80 mm

ing on guard; while another employed models variously used by Britains as Boer infantry and American infantry of the Spanish-American War. After years of conjecture, it is now known that the United States firm purchased castings in bulk from Britains. Later figures were solid-cast, but also clearly derived from Britains models—although slightly smaller (just over 50 mm).

That the American Soldier Company intended its troops to be popgun fodder is abundantly clear in its various sets entitled "Battle Game" and "Military Game" (a variation of Britains' Set No. 149, "American Soldiers"). In the latter, the toy soldiers could be set up on a special tray, patented by C. W. Beiser (who was treasurer and codirector of the company), and then knocked over by a child marksman armed with a popgun rifle provided in the set. (By tilting the tray, the figures could be made to snap back up.) According to the illustrated instruction card, a player earned five points if he hit a mounted officer, three for flag-bearers and musicians, and one for a lowly private. The sharpshooter who first toppled 50-points' worth of metal warriors was the winner.

Information about the years in which the American Soldier Company remained operational is sketchy, but it is generally believed that production began in the 1890s and continued until the 1920s. The only dates known with certainty are those relating to the special cardboard display tray invented by C. W. Beiser and patented first in England in 1904 and then in Germany and the United States in 1905. Interestingly, another type of Beiser tray appears in toy soldier sets from the Eureka Metal Company, also located in Brooklyn. Issued under the trademark Eureka American Soldiers, the sets, like those of the American Soldier Company, contained Britains-type figures, and the box label boasted that the Beiser tray was "the only tray in the world that displays soldiers in a standing and natural position without the aid of thread or wire." Given the proximity of the two firms, as well as their use of similar figures and display boards, some relationship may have existed between Eureka and the American Soldier Company. However, this has not been firmly established.

In the early decades of the 20th century, the Saint Louis Soldier Company joined the ranks of American copycat firms. Figures were issued in various sizes and were both fully and semiround. Company owner S. Chichester Lloyd crowed that his models were superior in quality to those "turned out by the million in British factories." But investigators have found that the firm's range was largely a mélange of recast Britains and Heydes, while others appear to have been clones of Reka, Haffner, and Schneider models. J. G. Garratt asserts that Mr. Lloyd confessed to having obtained many of his molds from German sources. At any rate, the figures were undistinguished and the firm faded away into well-deserved oblivion in the early 1920s.

Slightly more interesting are the toy soldiers produced by the Ideal Toy Company of Bridgeport, Connecticut. Beginning in the early 1920s, Ideal put out a line of American soldiers, sailors, marines, and Indians. Made from bronze molds obtained in Germany and sold to Lewis Christie, Ideal's owner, by another Bridgeport resident, the figures were hollow-casts, roughly 54 millimeters high, and were usually fitted with Britains-like movable arms.

Like other early American soldier firms, Ideal did not bother to place identification marks on its models. However, they are distinguishable by a rather thick oval base that slopes upward. According to a surviving member of the Christie family, the soldiers were sold in sets through several major New York City department stores. In addition to the hollow-casts, a few 40-millimeter solids are known to have been manufactured by Ideal. Simplistic in design, and based on molds of foreign manufacture, Ideal's range does represent a worthy effort at producing a distinctively American toy soldier for the American market. The company's toy soldier operation came to an end around 1929; but the molds survived until World War

A white-uniformed ski trooper typifies the heroic posturing of
Barclay military types.
Larry Levine Collection   Height: 80 mm

An American Legion officer by Barclay,
showing the characteristic half-moon eyelid
with a dot in the center.
Larry Levine Collection   Height: 80 mm

Cops and robbers have always captivated youngsters, and dime-store companies included policemen in their lines. From left to right, a Manoil police officer, a Barclay traffic cop, and a Barclay motorcycle officer.
Larry Levine Collection

Height: 80 mm

II, when they were gobbled up by the scrap metal drives and, as Henry Anton has whimsically observed, probably were "tossed back, in one form or another, at the Germans who originally made them."

It was not until the 1930s, however, that the United States developed uniquely American toy soldiers. Distinct in appearance from their European cousins, they were sold mainly as individual pieces in the ubiquitous "five-and-dime stores," especially the F. W. Woolworth chain, and so came to be known as dime-store soldiers. Rugged and robust, the dime-store doughboys stood a head taller than Britains and Mignots, generally measuring $3\frac{1}{4}$ inches (roughly 80 mm), although some makers produced slightly smaller versions. Their uniqueness derived not only from their appearance but also their accessibility. Dime stores were scattered all over the map of America and, in contrast to the fancier department stores, children could visit them freely, unattended by their parents.

If Mignot's figures were the aristocrats of toy soldiers, and those of Britains and Heyde the miniatures of the middle class, then dime-store soldiers were the proletariat's playthings. Just about any child, except the poorest of the poor, could scrape together the five pennies needed to pluck a dime-store doughboy from one of the overflowing counter bins. And so, appropriately, it was left to the United States, which has always prided itself on its ability to break down class barriers, to produce the first truly classless toy soldier.

Dime-store figures were simple and functional. Only rarely did the companies that produced them venture beyond the drab khaki that became *de rigueur* for the combat infantryman of the 20th century. Britains and Mignot could fuss all they wanted to about accuracy of uniform detail in their parade-dress troops; such technical niceties were generally shrugged off by the dime-store firms. If a toy soldier looked reasonably like a soldier, it was a soldier. With little variety in uniform, the dime-store doughboys made up for their drabness of hue with a multi-plicity of positions and functions that gave them a vitality found in few other toy soldiers. Until recently dime-store figures were sneered at as being rather vulgar by collectors of more sophisticated European types. But after decades of neglect, the dime-store figure has emerged as a collectible in its own right, with particularly rare pieces among what were once 5- and 10-cent toys selling for $100 or more. They are now appreciated, as one admirer has written, as "excellent examples of twentieth-century functional art."

Unfortunately, few prewar catalogues have survived, making it difficult to fully document the production lines and company histories of the various makers. But thanks to the diligent research efforts of Richard O'Brien, author of *Collecting Toys*, an indispensable reference guide to the subject, and of Don Pielen, we now have a fairly complete picture of who produced what. Space does not permit a comprehensive cataloguing of the hundreds of specific types turned out from the early 1930s to the end of the 1960s, but we can briefly sketch the histories of the major companies and offer some guidelines for identifying their figures.

The Barclay Manufacturing Company, named after the street in West Hoboken, New Jersey, where it was located, was the largest and best known of the dime-store firms. Founded in 1924 by a Frenchman named Léon Donze, an experienced toy maker, and an American businessman named Michael Levy, the company first produced a few standard-size (54 mm) toy soldiers, complete with movable arms, that had an obvious Britains influence in styling. Starting around 1934 or 1935, Barclay brought out the first of a long line of $3\frac{1}{4}$-inch hollow-cast figures. Designed by Frank Krupp, they were sturdy and heroic in their demeanor but failed to convey a sense of animation. These early figures are referred to by collectors as "short stride" because the legs of the marching soldiers are close together, giving them a rather stiff look. An improved version, more realistic in appearance and known as "long stride," went on sale in 1937.

A Barclay detective (right) flashes his badge as he apprehends a robber.
Larry Levine Collection   Height: 80 mm

A Barclay bride and groom take their nuptial vows before a
minister.
Larry Levine Collection

Height: 80 mm

In addition to its military figures, Barclay issued civilian types like these Boy Scouts.
Larry Levine Collection

Height: 80 mm

Barclay's prewar figures are easily recognized by their separately cast World War I–style tin helmets, which were first glued on and later, when chain stores complained that they frequently came off, were attached to the head by means of a clip. Barclays can also be recognized by their distinctive eyes. In the early 1930s, the eye consisted of a half-moon eyelid with a dot for a pupil at one end—making it look like a reclining comma. The dot was shifted to the center of the half moon around 1935, remaining that way until the last stages of the company's production.

Early Barclays carried no identifying marks on the figures or under the bases. Later, when other companies entered the field, figures were marked with the firm's name, an identifying number, and the words "Made in USA." The numbers related to the type of figure; for example, the 600s were civilian figures, the 700s military, while the 900s were initially reserved for "duplex" (two-piece) figures like the radio operator with a separate antenna mast that plugged into the radio.

The range of figures consisted mainly of American soldiers marching or in various combat poses—some firing, charging, or clubbing with rifles, others handling machine, antiaircraft, or antitank guns—as well as a smaller group of civilian types. Among the latter were cowboys and Indians, railroad passengers and station personnel, an interesting group of ice skaters and other winter figures, several Santa Clauses, and a man and woman seated in a one-horse open sleigh. Other novelty types included a detective with gun who could be pitted against a burglar, and a bride and groom with a minister performing the marriage ceremony. Occasionally the company issued topical lines such as Italian and Ethiopian combatants at the time of Mussolini's invasion of Ethiopia, and Chinese and Japanese soldiers during the 1937 Manchurian campaign.

That Barclay's figures enjoyed enormous popularity is indicated by the expansion of the work force from a few dozen in 1934 to 400 just before World War II, by which time the firm was turning out several million slush-molded castings a year. Around that time, Olive Kooken became the principal designer, replacing Frank Krupp, who had left to form his own company, All-Nu. Under Kooken's direction, the old tin-hatted troops were replaced by "cast-helmet" soldiers—pieces in which the helmet was cast as an integral part of the figure.

During World War II, Barclay, like other metal toy soldier makers, suspended operations. When production resumed after the war, the figures were gradually reduced in size, their stands eventually being discarded in favor of what became known as "pod feet" (really a small round base under each foot). The pod-foot series, begun in the 1950s, included a new range of GI's in updated World War II uniforms and helmets and using modern weapons such as tommy guns and bazookas. There was also a "mini-series" of railroad figures scaled to the popular HO-gauge toy trains. The company never enjoyed the same success after the war that it had in the 1930s, due in part to competition from plastic figures and Japanese imports, and the number of employees steadily declined. When the company finally closed its doors in 1971, the last major American maker to do so, fewer than 75 employees were still on the payroll.

Barclay's greatest rival in the toy soldier field—the company also produced vehicles and other toys—was Manoil, originally located in New York City and later in upstate New York. The firm was owned by two brothers, Jack and Maurice Manoil, with Jack providing the creative spark and Maurice handling day-to-day business operations. From 1928 to 1934, the company name was Man-O-Lamp Corporation, the product line consisting of metal lamps and novelty items sold through the chain stores. A major expansion of its toy-making operations began in 1934, the year its name was changed to Manoil Manufacturing Company.

All of Manoil's dime-store soldiers, first issued in 1935, were designed by Walter Baetz, an exceptionally gifted sculptor whose talented hands produced what are

At the time of the Italian invasion of
Ethiopia, Barclay issued Italian
infantrymen like the one shown above.
Larry Levine Collection Height: 80 mm

An extremely rare Barclay Ethiopian
Warrior ready to do battle.
Larry Levine Collection Height: 80 mm

Among the rarer Barclays is this Chinese
infantryman.
Larry Levine Collection   Height: 80 mm

With the coming of World War II, Barclay
produced a Japanese infantry figure.
Larry Levine Collection   Height: 80 mm

A Manoil deep-sea diver with full gear (left) and his Barclay
counterpart.
Larry Levine Collection   Height: 80 mm

perhaps the most distinctive dime-store figures. Vital, jaunty, often with a somewhat Oriental look, they have an air of caricature about them—for example, a parachutist landing with a thud on his rear end—that became more noticeable as the years went by. Indeed, many of the postwar GI figures, including those shown in energetic and exaggerated action stances and others in casual poses, evoke memories of Bill Mauldin's GI cartoon characters, Willie and Joe.

Initially, the toy soldier line was a predictable mix of soldiers, sailors, marines, and cowboys and Indians. But unlike Barclay, which maintained a blend of civilian and military figures, Manoil soon settled into an almost exclusively military range. Actually the decision was made by the chain stores, which dictated the production runs by their acceptance or rejection of prototype models brought to them for approval. Once the stores agreed to stock a given selection of figures, Manoil would begin manufacturing them. From the following account by Terry Sells, we learn how this was accomplished.

The figures would be sculpted in clay. The clay figure would be used to make a plaster mould and the plaster mould would then be cast in bronze. The bronze mould was next fitted with an ejector and mounted in an adjustable steel cradle. The cradle had a built-in lever which allowed the mould to open and close. When opened all the way, the ejector would be engaged, leaving the casting suspended between the mould halves. On either end of the cradle were posts on which the cradle would swivel, allowing the mould to be inverted. With this efficient device, a master and his assistant could turn out hundreds of castings daily. Flash was then cleaned from the castings by means of a die press. These innovations, along with design improvements in the moulds, made Manoil very competitive.

Because Walter Baetz was concerned with designing

molds that would produce a nearly break-proof soldier—or at least one that would remain whole until it reached the retail outlets—he often redesigned molds, with the result that about one-third of Manoil's pre–World War II figures have structural variations, some distinctive, others quite subtle. However, identifying Manoil figures presents no great problem. Most of the early models are marked with the name of the company and an identifying number. Around 1940, the letters and numbers were reduced in size, and the Manoil trademark, an "M" in a circle, was added, along with the words "Made in U.S.A." Some Manoil figures had no markings, but as Richard O'Brien points out, "they are distinctively enough like the others so that the eye can be quickly trained to recognize them." In contrast to the more ornate Barclay eye, Manoils were outfitted with a simple black line with a dot underneath.

Responding to pacifist pressures in the late 1930s, which led some stores to boycott military toys, Manoil brought out a series of civilian figures under the heading "The Happy Farm." All manner of farm and country folk were available, and one could select figures from among 40 different types. Farmers sowed grain, harvested with a scythe, and pitched hay, while their womenfolk churned butter, cooked, did the wash, and performed other domestic chores. There was also a variety of laborers—bricklayers, hod carriers, carpenters, blacksmiths—all busily at work.

By the late 1930s, Manoil had outgrown its Manhattan quarters. Expansion to meet growing demand forced it to move first to Brooklyn in 1937 and then to Waverly, New York, in 1940, where it occupied a spacious facility of some 45,000 square feet. Here 225 workers, mostly women and high school students, cleaned, painted, and assembled the castings. In the months preceding America's entry into World War II, as much as 60 tons of metal were required weekly to produce several hundred thousand toys.

After a wartime suspension (except for a brief effort to produce composition figures), Manoil reopened at the

A squad of Barclay fire fighters.
Larry Levine Collection   Height: 80 mm

Designed by Walter Baetz, Manoil figures, like these GI boxers,
showed more expressiveness than other dime-store doughboys.
Larry Levine Collection   Height: 80 mm

Nowhere is the Manoil sense of humor better displayed than in this figure of a parachuting pilot crash-landing on his rump.
Larry Levine Collection   Height: 80 mm

end of 1945. A new line of GI's in World War II battle dress followed, but the company never regained its prewar popularity or production levels. The firm hobbled along until the mid-1950s, finally closing shortly after the death of Jack Manoil, in 1955.

Third among the major dime-store makers was Grey Iron of Mount Joy, Pennsylvania, which has existed since 1840 under various names, first as a machine shop and later, beginning in 1903, as a manufacturer of toys. It was the only dime-store company that produced cast-iron toy soldiers. In 1917, shortly after the United States entered World War I, the firm brought out its "Greyklip Armies," a series of 40-millimeter nickel-plated troops costing a modest 10 cents for a carded set of 10 infantry or 5 cavalry. Dressed in the campaign hats and puttees worn by American soldiers of the early 1900s, the figures were "klipped" by means of a tin-strip device to an illustrated backing card that featured a scene showing troops in the field. In 1938, the 40-millimeter line was modernized under the heading "Uncle Sam's Defenders" and consisted of a parade set in "Montana" campaign hats and a steel-helmeted action set with machine gunners. In contrast to "Greyklip Armies," the new sets were painted doughboy khaki, sometimes with splashes of flesh color on hands and faces to give a further touch of realism.

Three-inch dime-store soldiers were issued by Grey Iron in 1933; the roster included a group of American Revolutionary War soldiers, along with West Point cadets and a selection of doughboys marching and in action. By mid-1936, the firm was distributing its "Iron Men" series, which were better designed than earlier models. The new figures stood a full 3¼ inches, bringing them into line with those of Barclay and Manoil, their principal competitors. Probably because of the material used to make them, Grey Iron's soldiers were simple in design and certainly the least imaginative in pose of all the dime-store figures. "The soldiers were hand-poured and then painted on an assembly-line basis," reports Richard O'Brien, "and at least initially were sold for a dime, while their com-

petitors charged a nickel."

The company did produce an interesting civilian range called "The American Family" that featured 54-millimeter figures—the proper scale for 0-gauge trains. Among the five sets in the series were "The American Family Travels" and "The American Family on the Beach." The latter had a most unusual assortment of civilian types, mostly in bathing suits. Included were a man lying on the sand with a newspaper over his face; a lifeguard perched on his lookout chair; a boy playing with a beach ball; a little girl with a sand pail; and such essential scenic props as a lifeboat, a cabana, and a section of boardwalk.

Grey Iron survived the postwar doldrums that finished off most of the dime-store companies, and even produced a new group of American Continental soldiers in the 1950s. However, the toy soldier part of the business was never revived in any meaningful way after the war. Nevertheless, the company remains in business today (a division of the Donsco Corporation), producing mechanical banks and other cast-iron toys.

The fourth major producer of dime-store soldiers was the Auburn Rubber Company of Auburn, Indiana, which got its start in 1913 as the Double Fabric Tire Corporation, a major supplier of rubber tires and tubes for Mr. Ford's "Model T" cars. In 1935, now operating as Auburn, the firm entered the toy soldier field with a modest assortment of five different figures, one of them patterned after a miniature palace guard the company's president had acquired while on a trip to England. As the company name suggests, Auburn's figures were made of rubber, the only dime-store soldiers manufactured from this material. Large rubber presses, each containing 40 to 60 figures, were used to mold the figures. Once trimmed and coated with a vegetable dye lacquer, the rubber men were placed on a conveyor apparatus that ran them by several dozen women who deftly brush-painted faces, footgear, buttons, and belts, as well as other touches that brought them to life.

Auburn concentrated on military figures, producing

Manoil doughboys at target practice. The foreground figure is a rare version with a rifle that snaps down.
Larry Levine Collection
Height: 80 mm

Dime-store doughboys by Manoil relaxing in camp.
Larry Levine Collection   Height: 80 mm

A headquarters unit with both Barclay and Manoil figures.
Larry Levine Collection   Height: 80 mm

virtually no civilians except for a well-designed group of baseball and football players. These diminutive athletes, issued around 1940, represent the culmination of an evolutionary process that saw the first fragile figures of the mid-1930s steadily develop through improved design into the heftier and better-proportioned fellows produced just before World War II. Auburn also devoted considerable effort to promotion and packaging. Advertisements of its line, sometimes in several colors, were prominently displayed in leading toy trade periodicals such as *Playthings* and *Toys and Novelties*; and, at least in this area of promotion, Auburn clearly outgeneraled its major rivals—Barclay, Manoil, and Grey Iron. Similarly, Auburn scored a significant packaging triumph in 1940, when its boxed set of 18 baseball players captured the Grand Prize at the third annual toy-packaging contest. (The firm beat out such high-powered competition as Parker Brothers.)

Auburn also made clever use of its boxes to knock the opposition. When consumer-advocate groups warned parents in the mid-1930s about the dangers to children posed by metal toys—particularly soldiers with high lead content—Auburn proclaimed the virtues of rubber models. Boxes were emblazoned with such messages as "Protect the Child While Playing" and "Sanitary, Noiseless, Washable.... Will Not Scratch Fingers, Floors or Furniture." Furthermore, kids would have a devil of a time destroying these resilient rubber fellows: "Bounce 'em! Drop 'em! Squeeze 'em! Throw 'em! They just can't break!"

Unfortunately, they did bend, tilt, and lean, often precariously teetering on their stands. Their rubber construction also meant that they were not as finely detailed as their metal compatriots. Probably for these reasons, Auburn's toy troops—as well as their vehicles and other toys—are not much sought after by collectors, although they enjoyed enormous popularity in their heyday. Rubber being almost as important to the war effort as metal, toy soldier production stopped after Pearl Harbor. During the postwar years, some toy soldiers were produced, including several new plastic models; but, for the most part, the company concentrated on other toys. Auburn's toy division was purchased by a New Mexico concern in 1960 and ended its activities in 1969.

Because of their rarity, the products of some of the less-successful metal dime-store soldier manufacturers have become highly valued by collectors. The toy soldiers of All-Nu, owned by former Barclay sculptor Frank Krupp, are probably the rarest. They are also extremely well designed, since Krupp was a professional artist who painstakingly sculpted each master out of ordinary clay placed over a wire armature. Krupp's imaginative figures included an army newsreel cameraman; showing a helmeted soldier kneeling behind a large movie camera mounted on a tripod; a spirited group of "Marching Majorettes," also known as the "All-Girl Band," with four instrumentalists, a flag-bearer, and two prancing, baton-twirling majorettes; and several nicely animated football players. All-Nu was in business from 1938 to 1941 but probably did not turn to soldier making until 1940. The firm's soldiers and most of its other figures have the company name stamped on the underbase.

Tommy Toy, of Union City, New Jersey, which made its first sale on November 13, 1935, is another of these worthy but short-lived companies. Among those involved in its early operations was Léon Donze, one of Barclay's cofounders, and one of its designers was Olive Kooken, who later became the principal Barclay sculptor. With cross-fertilization such as this fairly common in the dime-store figure fraternity, it is understandable that, to an untrained eye, one dime-store soldier looks like another. Thirteen known toy soldier models were manufactured, each marked "Tommy Toy" under the base, to which is added, in some cases, a description of the figure—for example, "Officer Gas Mask." Even more interesting, and slightly more common than its soldiers, is the firm's series of ten nursery rhyme figures, with such favorites as Old Mother Hubbard, Little Bo Peep, and Jack and the Beanstalk. The company, which was not successful, is believed to have gone out of business around 1939. American Alloy,

Listed in the Manoil catalogue only as "General," this pistol-packing
four-star general was obviously inspired by America's most colorful
World War II field commander, General George S. Patton, Jr.
Larry Levine Collection   Height: 80 mm

The wide range of Medical Corps figures produced by the dime-
store companies can be seen in this grouping of Barclay and Manoil
models.
Larry Levine Collection   Height: 80 mm

A Manoil ski trooper.
Larry Levine Collection   Height: 80 mm

a copycat firm, reproduced Tommy Toy's soldiers from new master molds, first in 1941 and then briefly after the war. These are easily distinguishable from original Tommy Toys by the lack of markings on the underbase.

During World War II, when metal was restricted and most dime-store firms shut their doors, three companies began manufacturing 3¼-inch composition figures to fill the gap. Until recently, the first company remained shrouded in mystery. Thanks to the detective work of Richard O'Brien, we now know that the firm was called Molded Products and that it was officially incorporated at the end of 1941 by a father-and-son team, Leslie Steinau and Leslie, Jr.

With the aid of Irving Reader, former chief salesman for Barclay, equipment was purchased and installed in a Manhattan building. Made from a mixture of wood flour (fine-ground sawdust), starch, and water, the figures were quickly gobbled up by dime stores hungry for any kind of toy soldiers. At least 14 types were sold (generally priced at 7 cents apiece), including a cowboy, an Indian, a marine, a sailor, and assorted U.S. soldiers and aviators. Perfunctorily designed, they were mainly copies of other makers' figures; they are easily recognized by a hole in the middle of the base and another in the crotch, resulting from the impaling of the figures on nails attached to wooden boards during the drying process.

A second company, Playwood Plastics, also produced composition soldiers out of a mixture of fine-ground sawdust, borax, flour, and water. Playwood, which began turning out soldiers in mid-1944, was a subsidiary of Transogram, a major toy company. Nearly all of Playwood's figures, marked with a "P" within a triangle, were apparently based on Manoil models. Operating out of a Brooklyn, New York, factory, the company was successful for about a year, employing 125 people. But when the war ended and lead soldiers were available once again, composition figures were no longer competitive and so were discontinued.

In 1944, Manoil became the third composition-figure maker, using a fine-grained substance that included sulfur to make four models of soldiers and one of a tank. Generally considered the best designed of the American composition soldiers, they are now ardently sought as rarities by collectors. For the most part, however, the wartime composition soldiers suffered from flaws that reduced their durability. Specifically, they tended to break easily, often dissolved in water, and generally weathered poorly. Most were crudely sculpted and painted. But although unsatisfactory in the long run, composition figures filled a temporary need and, since they were the same size as the standard dime-store soldiers, fit nicely into the existing prewar lead, iron, and rubber armies of many American boys.

Although the dime-store doughboy was America's unique contribution to the world of the toy soldier, mention should be made of several firms that produced 54-millimeter figures during the same period. In 1929, the J. L. Wright Toy Company of Chicago, founded by the son of renowned American architect Frank Lloyd Wright, issued figures of American Indians to accompany its popular line of "Lincoln Log" frontier forts and cabins. Cowboys, pioneers, and Canadian Mounties followed soon after, marketed both as individual pieces and in assorted boxed sets—sometimes in combination with the assemble-your-self log forts and buildings.

Military figures began to appear in the mid-1930s and there seems to have been an ambitious plan to portray in miniature American military units from the Revolutionary War on down. Only a few of these actually materialized; among them were Continentals in tricorns, a mounted figure of George Washington, a War of 1812 infantryman, and some World War I doughboys. Other military types included a West Point cadet and a sailor in white cap and leggings. Box labels carried a statement asserting that the figures "were made from a new hard material which is practically unbreakable"—a claim quickly challenged and disproved by more aggressive youngsters.

With toy trains becoming the rage, Wright added a set

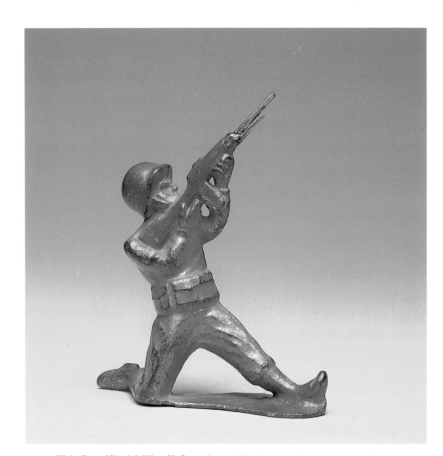

This Post-World War II American infantryman demonstrates the
dynamic posing of Manoil's military figures.
Larry Levine Collection   Height: 80 mm

At the time of America's entry into World War I, Grey Iron issued its first toy soldiers. Called the "Greyklip Armies," the series consisted of 40mm nickel-plated U. S. Army troops.
Larry Levine Collection

Height: Foot figures: 40 mm
Mounted: 45 mm

Unlike other dime-store figure makers, Grey Iron made
toy soldiers like this American sailor out of cast iron.
Larry Levine Collection   Height: 80 mm

of railroad personnel and passengers. Included were a redcap carrying a bag, a train engineer holding an oil can, a policeman clutching a nightstick, and several male passengers. Produced in large quantities, these are among the best-known American-made civilian figures. Top honors for originality, however, would surely go to a Lincoln Log set entitled "Og, Son of Fire." Based on a popular radio show of the day, the set featured a cast of early cave dwellers and wild beasts of the prehistoric past. Highly unusual to say the least; after all, how many toy soldier makers could boast of having a set with a tyrannosaur named Rex and a stegosaur named Three Horn?

The Wright Toy Company was taken over by the Playskool Manufacturing Company in 1942. Most of the prewar sets were discontinued after the war, but the railway people and a few other metal figures were issued by Playskool until the early 1950s. For identification purposes, Wright marked their figures "Lincoln Logs U.S.A.," a designation dropped after Playskool took over. Some early figures are marked "Noveltoy," which may be the imprint of a company owned or bought out by Wright.

For sheer perseverance, one would be hard pressed to find a toy soldier maker who could match the record of J. Edward Jones of Chicago. No manufacturer tried harder or failed more often than he. During the thirty-odd years that Jones was engaged in the business of producing toy troops, he left a trail of "false starts, unfulfilled hopes, comic-tragic incidents, and apocryphal stories," as Don Pielen observes. The Jones odyssey had its start in the mid-1920s, when he issued hollow-cast 54-millimeter troops from early American wars. In 1929, the year of the stock market crash, Jones founded his first company, Metal Art Miniatures, with predictable results. The company, which commissioned an English firm to do a series of original molds, went under in 1931.

Undaunted, Jones snapped back quickly with a new enterprise called the Miniature Products Company. Molds commissioned but unpaid for were now purchased at a reduced price from the English maker. Sketchy records indicate that among these were molds for U.S. cavalry from the Mexican War, Indian wars, and the Spanish–American War; infantry and cavalry from World War I, and a series of soldiers, sailors, and West Point cadets in 1930s dress. Miniature Products fared no better than its predecessor; it went out of business in 1936.

Toward the end of the 1930s, Jones—no doubt inspired by the success of Barclay and Manoil—turned his attention to the manufacture of dime-store (3¼-inch) figures, and he is known to have issued at least 30 different types. Some were thinly veiled copies of Barclay and Manoil models, and others were distinctively original—for example, a wounded soldier clutching his throat. Jones seems to have ended his dime-store line around 1940. By then he had formed yet another company, Metal Miniatures, in partnership with Ella Hume, who was both a financial backer and a figure designer. Metal restrictions and a stint in the navy disrupted this Jones operation and it, too, faded out.

In 1946, Jones bounced back under the heading Moulded Miniatures. From then until his death in 1957, he operated under a variety of names—Metal Arts, Universal, World Miniatures, Loyart, and Varifix among them—so that it must have seemed to the unknowing that he was a mini-conglomerate. He also found time to start something called the Visual Art Association and to edit, for a brief time, *Scabbard*, the journal of the Military Miniature Society of Illinois.

Sold singly and in boxed sets, Jones figures came in all sizes, shapes, and forms. Many were simplistic in design and paintwork, while some were of a fairly high standard. "Painting of Jones' 54-millimeter figures was done by a great variety of hands," explains Don Pielen, "sometimes with little supervision. Some early figures have blues and even reds with an almost iridescent hue; color variety and quality is comparable with imports. Other figures display an almost china-doll appearance. But there are few clues to a Jones figure in its paint style, animation or casting."

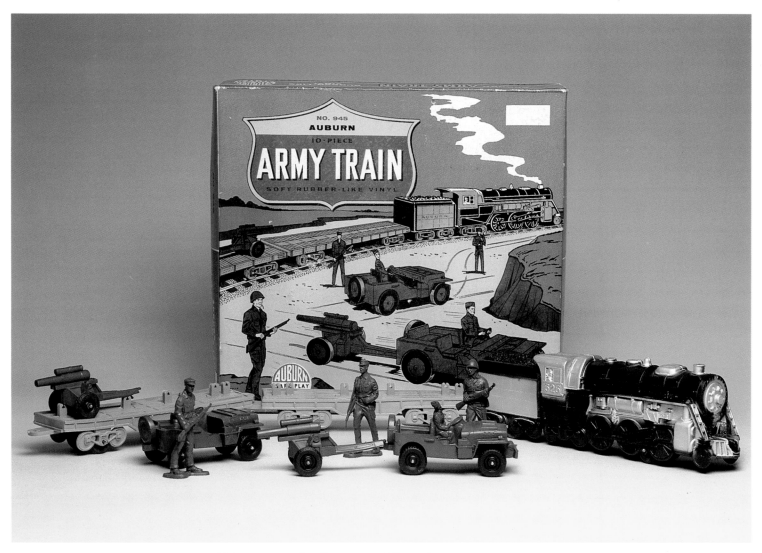

Unique among the dime-store soldier makers was the Auburn
Rubber Company, which produced toy soldiers and some civilian
types out of rubber. Here we see a selection of post-World War II
military figures and vehicles, and a model train.
Larry Levine Collection

In addition to its popular line of Lincoln Log frontier forts and cabins, the J. L. Wright Toy Company of Chicago also turned out a limited series of toy soldiers, cowboys and Indians, and frontiersmen—like the one shown above.
Steve Balkin Collection   Height: 54 mm

During a somewhat checkered career of more than thirty years, J. Edward Jones turned out toy soldiers of every shape and size under a variety of trade names. Among his earliest figures were soldiers of the American Revolutionary War, including this British grenadier.
Henry Kurtz Collection   Height: 54 mm

Prompted by the success of dime-store companies like Barclay and Manoil, J. Edward Jones issued a series of dime-store figures in the late 1930s. One of the earliest was a model of an American infantry officer.

Larry Levine Collection   Height: 80 mm

Nor were there any markings to serve as a guide. Except for a few early figures marked "Made in Chicago," the bases are blank. Different designers were employed at different times, so there is no consistency of style. During his three decades of activity, Jones produced figures of 40, 54, 75, and 80 millimeters. There was even a special "showcase" range of 6-inch (15 cm) models. It is not surprising then that, confronted with an American figure of unknown manufacture, collectors will often shrug and say "It's probably a Jones." Despite an unparalleled record of failures and partial successes, Jones deserves to be kindly remembered. He was innovative and imaginative, possibly the first American maker to issue soldiers of the American Revolutionary War; and despite mishaps, the Great Depression, and a major war, he refused to admit defeat, giving added meaning to the old adage about trying and trying again even if at first you don't succeed.

Among the rarest and the finest American toy soldiers are those of the short-lived company that operated under the trade name "The Warren Lines." Brooklyn-born John Warren, Jr., founder of the firm, went into production around 1935 with a series of U. S. cavalrymen in the khaki service uniforms of the period. Initially, the horses were hollow-cast, while the detachable riders were solid. When sculptress Margaret Cloninger—who also designed many of the Tommy Toy figures—joined the firm, a new range of spirited and anatomically superior solid-cast mounts was created. (Having found an excellent modeler in Miss Cloninger, Warren sensibly married the lady.)

Without doubt, Warren's toy troopers are the most superbly crafted U. S. cavalrymen turned out by an American maker. Horses came in seven positions, from standing and walking to cantering, galloping, and prancing. Troopers on galloping mounts are hunched over their horses' necks, conveying a realistic sense of a hell-for-leather cavalry charge. To offset the drab khaki dress of the soldiers, horses were painted in a rainbow of colors; and the troopers held pistols, sabers, rifles, or troop

guidons and regimental standards in their hands.

Infantry figures came in a variety of stances: at attention, marching, charging, or in action as skirmishers. Buglers, drummers, and flag-bearers were provided for all the groups except the skirmishers. Enlisted men carried rifles, sometimes with fixed bayonets, sometimes without, while the officers were equipped with pistols or swords. Rounding out the infantry was a machine-gun section that featured Browning 30-caliber machine guns either mounted on a tripod or on a wheeled carriage with a seated gunner. Infantrymen carried full field equipment, including backpacks and ammunition pouches, while officers sported Sam Browne belts and high boots, as opposed to the puttees of the enlisted men.

Surely the highlight of the Warren Lines was a marvelous horse artillery gun team comprising a cannon with lever-action firing mechanism, a limber, and either a four- or six-horse team. "A quick glance [at this set] encourages comparison to the Britains steel-helmeted artillery sets of the same vintage," writes Warren authority Steve Balkin. "A closer look, however, is more likely to bring to mind the horse furniture of early Lucottes, or the bulk and animation of large-size Heydes. The Warren product draws from all these antecedents, but the result is unique and dramatic." Gunners were seated on the limber, and the cannon provided additional seats for cannoneers on the trail and sometimes on the front of the shield. Mounted outriders, officers, dispatch riders, and flag-bearers also could be obtained.

Warren figures are slightly larger than Britains and Mignots—about 60 millimeters. Continental-style plug-in heads enabled the firm to issue its soldiers with either regulation parade-ground peaked caps or shrapnel-proof helmets. Seat pegs in the Heyde manner were used to secure mounted soldiers to their horses. Most figures had two movable arms. By 1937, Warrens were being sold, both individually boxed and in sets, in several New York, Philadelphia, and Baltimore department stores. Priced somewhat higher than the figures of their dime-store com-

Particularly rare is this kneeling Germany infantryman by J. Edward
Jones.
Larry Levine Collection   Height: 56 mm

A troop of Warren cavalrymen with regimental flags and company guidon charges into battle. Many collectors regard these toy troopers as the finest U. S. cavalrymen produced by an American maker.
Burtt Ehrlich Collection   Height: 85 mm

Warren's superb U. S. Field Artillery unit galloping into action.
Burtt Ehrlich Collection   Height: Mounted figures: 85 mm

petitors—averaging 15 cents for foot figures and 35 cents for mounted troops—Warrens did not fare well in the marketplace. Lagging sales forced John Warren to abandon his venture in 1939, bringing to an end a line of figures that, in the words of one commentator, exhibited "a craftsmanship uncommon to American toy soldiers."

In 1941, Warren sold off the remaining stock of his well-designed cavalry horses to the Comet Metal Products Company, which was then involved in producing its own line of toy soldiers. Some twenty years earlier, Comet had begun operations as a die-casting firm under the direction of founder Abraham Slonim. Having devised a time-saving centrifugal casting apparatus in the 1930s, Slonim and his sons, Joseph and Samuel, looked for new ways to employ it. Toy soldiers being a popular item, the Slonims started a line they called "The Brigadiers" shortly before World War II. Billed as "Authentic Models of Soldiers of the World," the toy troops, which did indeed range across the globe and the span of history, were mainly close cousins of Britains models, complete with movable arms. Their only truly original qualities were the distinctive base, a stubby, oval affair sprouting squared-off projections at both ends, and the rather pronounced forward lean of some charging models, whimsically dubbed "the deep-knee bend."

With the outbreak of war in Europe, Comet began angling for a U. S. government contract to produce small-scale identification models of warships, military vehicles, and aircraft. The Japanese attack on Pearl Harbor brought those efforts to fruition, and within a few days after America's entry into the war, the Comet plant in Richmond Hill, New York, was running on a round-the-clock seven-day schedule producing scale models for the War Department. A retrospective *New York Times* article (September 13, 1959) noted that "from 1941–45 Comet produced more than 10,000,000 models of defense items."

It was during this period of profits from government contracts that Comet formed its "Swedish Connection." Enter Curt Wennberg, a reserve officer in the Swedish Army, reactivated in 1940 and sent to the United States as a military attaché. Wennberg had been associated earlier with Fred Winkler, a German fugitive from Nazi Germany, whom Wennberg had assisted in immigrating to Great Britain. There, in 1935, Winkler established Treforest Mouldings, a firm that produced scale models of Napoleonic-period warships, and later some 40- to 45-millimeter miniature soldiers. Wennberg was engaged by Winkler to design some of the ship models. Probably because of this background, Wennberg was put in contact with Comet shortly after his arrival in the United States and may have designed some of their ID models.

Such is the background for one of the most interesting stories in toy soldier annals, a truly international endeavor that moves from the United States to Sweden, to Ireland, and eventually to South Africa. It begins at war's end with Comet, flush with profits from government work and encouraged by Curt Wennberg, reviving its prewar interest in toy soldiers. Wennberg suggested that a fellow Swede named Holger Eriksson be employed to design a new line of toy warriors of the world. The choice could not have been better, for in Holger Eriksson, Comet obtained the services of one of the world's foremost creators of miniature soldiers.

A draftsman by profession, Eriksson began making finely detailed model soldiers for his own pleasure in the mid-1930s, working first in wood and later in metal. Accepting the Comet commission, he now brought his considerable talent and meticulous craftsmanship to the task of designing toy soldiers. In short order, Eriksson fashioned more than 200 masters in 55 millimeters and a few in 40 millimeters. His method, as he explained at the time in a letter to an American friend, was to carve the basic figure out of modeler's wax. Next came a plaster mold, from which, using an alloy of half tin and half lead, the first metal figures were cast. The extra tin content kept the metal soft enough for Eriksson to further refine the figure by carving extra detail and adding what he termed "individual expression."

The excellent animation of Warren's galloping and cantering horses
shows up clearly in this view of infantry and cavalry on the move.
Burtt Ehrlich Collection

Height: Foot figures: 60 mm
Mounted: 85 mm

A squad of Warren infantrymen, including machine gunners, deploys
for action.
Burtt Ehrlich Collection   Height: 60 mm

Before producing its better-known Authenticast lines, the Comet
Metal Products Company issued a range of toy soldiers under the
heading "The Brigadiers." Most of the figures, like these French
infantrymen, were plagiarized Britains designs.
Ernest Schwartz Collection   Height: 54 mm

The result was a series of toy soldiers that have no match in their realistic portrayal of fighting men. Eriksson's creations have a rough-hewn, naturalistic look and an ease of movement that is most obvious in the action figures. His foot soldiers are anatomically faultless and his beautifully sculpted horses are properly proportioned. Whether one is looking at a 16th-century pikeman standing at the ready—in a pose taken directly from a military manual of the day—or a kneeling World War II German soldier rearing back to toss a grenade, the work of a master craftsman is always evident. One can only agree with Steve Sommers's assessment: "The artistic qualities of Eriksson masters can show through bad painting and poor casting. Unlike the fine details of Britains' castings, lost beneath a single coat of paint, or the reserved, don't touch, work of art look of many Mignots, the best of Eriksson's work for Authenticast was art to be played with."

While Eriksson worked on his masters, Comet ironed out the production details. Casting was to be done at the New York plant, with the figures then being shipped in bulk to a factory in Ireland set up by Wennberg. At first only painting was handled at the Irish factory, located in a section of Galway called Claddagh, and the figures were then returned to the United States for boxing and distribution. Later, all work was done in Ireland, while Comet's New York facility handled North American distribution. Wennberg also arranged to have Fred Winkler—who had just set up a new firm called Malleable Mouldings at Deal, England—supervise sales in Great Britain and Continental Europe.

Production in Ireland began in the last months of 1946, and by early 1947 boxed sets were appearing on the shelves of American and British toy stores. Comet issued its figures in sturdy red boxes under the trademark Authenticast–Comet Gaeltacht Industries. A standard red, white, and blue label, featuring line drawings of warriors and soldiers from ancient times to World War II, was used on all boxes. At one end of the label were the words "History in Miniature" and the Authenticast trademark.

Under the line drawings appeared the motto "The Finest Models Ever Built," which, in this case, was only a slight exaggeration.

An early catalogue lists nearly 200 different sets in the fully round 55-millimeter series. The British Empire and France accounted for over 100, while both Germany and the United States were each allotted 25 entries. Another ten nations received attention, among them Russia, Sweden, Poland, Austria, Hungary, Spain, China, and Italy. European troops ranged from 17th-century pikemen and musketeers to soldiers of World War II, with the Napoleonic Wars and the two world wars receiving the most coverage. There were French colonial troops, including colorful Turcos and Zouaves struggling under the weight of heavy field packs, and British Indian Army units in dress and service uniforms. Nearly all of the wars of the United States were covered, with Revolutionary War Continentals, Georgia Riflemen, and scouts in beaver hats and fringed buckskin jackets; Northern and Southern troops of the Civil War; World War I doughboys (including troops from the Philippine Islands); and a large selection of marines and infantrymen in assorted poses from World War II. All carried the monogram "HE" (for Holger Eriksson) and the word "Eire" under the bases, which were of many shapes—sometimes consisting of only a slender strip of metal with a cross-piece to provide balance.

The 40-millimeter semiround range, consisting mainly of figures cast from old bronze molds owned by Wennberg, with a few new models designed by Eriksson, never really got off the ground. Badly cast and poorly painted, they quickly went off the market. A pity, too, because the catalogue lists such enticing sets as an Austrian engineer work party from World War I, a German Army marching band of World War II, and a Japanese light coast artillery unit of the same period. Many more nations were represented than in the 55-millimeter range, including such generally neglected countries as Czechoslovakia, Mexico (three entries),

A Swedish Army Color Guard by Authenticast, with a superb
Eriksson figure of the color bearer with flag extended.
Henry Kurtz Collection   Height: 55 mm

Rough-hewn and rugged in appearance, this Authenticast Australian
infantryman is a prime example of the work of Swedish master
modeler Holger Eriksson, who designed more than 200 masters for
Comet's Authenticast line of toy soldiers.
Ernest Schwartz Collection   Height: 55 mm

The superb action qualities of Eriksson's figures is nowhere more
evident than in this group of World War II Authenticast British
infantrymen.
Ernest Schwartz Collection   Height: 55 mm

Rumania, Switzerland, Spain (six entries including Civil Guards and Moroccans), Turkey (three entries), and Yugoslavia. Among civilian types were Boy Scouts, football and soccer players, and railway and farm figures. Only the railroad figures, sculpted by Eriksson and a resident Comet designer named Frank Rogers, appear to have survived; they were still on the Comet list until the end of the 1950s.

On the whole, the Authenticast venture did not prove successful. Throughout the late 1940s, the 55-millimeter line was available in many American and European department stores and specialty shops. In New York, for example, they were carried by Macy's, where a boxed set of six or seven pieces was sold for only 98 cents—way under the price of a typical Britains set, which averaged about $1.75 during the same period. But despite the superior quality of the figures and competitive prices, Authenticasts did not capture a wide audience. Production was spotty and dealers complained of long delays in receiving orders. The quality of casting and painting, originally of a fairly high standard, began to decline noticeably. The final blow came in 1950, when a fire completely destroyed the Irish factory. Wennberg managed to salvage some of the molds and, joined by Fred Winkler, relocated to South Africa, where the two men founded a company called Swedish African Engineers (S.A.E.).

Under an arrangement with Eriksson, they reissued many of the Authenticast figures and also produced new models designed by the Swedish master.

Back in the United States, Comet sold off its existing stock of Authenticast sets and then began issuing unpainted castings of the Eriksson models for a burgeoning group of hobbyists interested in painting their own miniatures. The firm continued to manufacture its small-scale identification models and railroad figures until the early 1960s, when its metal models were swept off the market by the rising tide of plastic toys. So ended the noble but ill-fated Authenticast venture, which, as an article in the *Old Toy Soldier Newsletter* put it, "must be given top honours for combining gall and internationalism in toy soldier production."

Comet's Authenticast line represents the last serious effort by an American maker to create a quality range of traditional toy soldiers. When Barclay cooled its molds for the last time in 1971, the American metal toy soldier was no more. Like their British, French, and German cousins, the McLoughlins, Barclays, Manoils, Warrens, and Authenticasts have gone to those Valhallas reserved for toy troops that have faithfully performed their playtime duties. Artifacts of an earlier, perhaps simpler time, they are now valued as collectibles and treasured as nostalgic mementos.

These World War II German infantrymen
are typical of Holger Eriksson's action figures.
Ernest Schwartz Collection   Height: 55 mm

An 18th-century infantryman by Authenticast.
Note the slender strip of metal that serves as a base.
Henry Kurtz Collection   Height: 55 mm

Authenticast figures ranged as far back as the 17th century and included such interesting historical types as these early English musketeers. A standard red, white, and blue box was used for all of the firm's sets.
Henry Kurtz Collection   Height: 55 mm

An Authenticast Dutch grenadier of the Napoleonic
Wars advances with steady determination.
Henry Kurtz Collection   Height: 55 mm

An 18th-century line-infantry drummer by Authenticast.
Henry Kurtz Collection   Height: 55 mm

French Army Turcos take up firing positions as they would have in a
desert encounter with North African tribesmen.
Ernest Schwartz Collection   Height: 55 mm

A squad of Authenticast Australian infantrymen on the march.
Ernest Schwartz Collection   Height: 55 mm

A rare Authenticast figure of a Japanese
marine of World War II.
Henry Kurtz Collection   Height: 55 mm

A Black Watch officer by Authenticast orders his men
into battle.
Ernest Schwartz Collection   Height: 55 mm

After the Authenticast factory in Ireland burned down, two of the
principals, Curt Wennberg and Fred Winkler, relocated to South
Africa, where they continued to produce toy soldiers under the
trade name Swedish African Engineers. Here we see a display set of
30mm figures depicting a Union Army encampment during the
American Civil War.
Ernest Schwartz Collection   Height: 30 mm

CHAPTER V
OTHER MAKERS
Soldiers of the World

Although Great Britain, France, Germany, and the United States were the major manufacturers of lead soldiers, firms in other countries also produced toy troops of superior quality—though usually on a much smaller scale. Given our focus on the principal makers of the "Big Four" nations, we can do little more than skip over the surface and offer a brief international tour of some of the more highly regarded of these firms.

Moving from south to north in Europe, we begin in Italy, where flat figures were made as early as the 1770s. Not until the 20th century, however, did three-dimensional figures make their appearance. Influenced by the success of Britains and Heyde, Francesco and Luciano Antonini began making standard-size metal models (roughly 54 mm) between the two world wars. Operating under the name FIGIR (an acronym for the jawbreaking Fabbrica Italiana Giocattoli Infangibili Roma), they concentrated on Italian troops of the 19th and 20th centuries, but also produced Napoleonics and ancient Romans. By and large, the figures are nicely designed and the standard of painting is fully comparable to that of Mignot. Their figures of the Bersaglieri advancing at the run are probably the most accurate toy soldier representations of this well-known Italian fighting unit. Weapons and equipment are separately cast and soldered onto the fixed-arm figures, which stand on ovalish bases, and riders are detachable from their mounts. The firm still produces figures in both metal and plastic.

Somewhat cruder in appearance are the figures of ISA (Industria Soprammobili Artistici), which began operations in Turin after World War II. Much more extensive in range than FIGIR's, the offerings of this firm include troops of many nations and historical periods (usually in boxes of three to six figures), with some interesting 17th- and 18th-century types. Both FIGIR and ISA models are well regarded in their native land and, as J. G. Garratt observes, they "are as popular in Italy as Britains are in England."

Across the Mediterranean in Spain, metal toy soldiers were first produced in the 1830s, when an Italian émigré named Carlos Ortelli Dotti established a workshop in Barcelona. At first religious and other civilian themes predominated, and there were charming scenes of flamenco dancers and peasants in colorful local costumes. Military figures were subsequently added; and by the end of the 19th century, thanks to Ortelli and his chief competitors, Pirozzini and Lleonart, Barcelona had become the Nuremberg of Spain—the center of a thriving toy soldier industry. So widely distributed were these early tin troops that, according to a Spanish historian, "Lead soldiers provided the main entertainment of many children, rich and poor, in Spain during the [19th] century."

In the 1890s, flat figures gave way to three-dimensional solids, most of which—like the more popular Heyde range—were 45 millimeters in height. In 1896, Baldomero Casanellas created an extensive line of toy soldiers under the trade name La Guerra. Military figures were issued in boxes of 10 to 64 pieces, and in addition to Spanish troops, the military forces of other major European countries were available in a wide range of poses. In later years, the firm was taken over by José Capell Coixet and is better known by the name Capell. Metal figures were replaced by plastics in the 1950s.

Other Spanish firms of note were Palomeque and Castresana, both based in Madrid, and Eulogio, Teo, and Jiménez, which operated in Barcelona. According to José

← Some of the charm of Old Vienna is captured by these Wollner figures of a gentleman and his lady out for a ride.
Henry Kurtz Collection   Height: 65 mm

Manuel Allendesálazar, a Spanish authority, all of these firms displayed "great ingenuity in reproducing not only military figures but also delightful scenes of peasants, town-dwellers, sportsmen, and, needless to say, bull-fighters in all possible attitudes." Virtually all of the Spanish firms surrendered to plastic in the 1940s and 1950s, and the earlier metal figures, like their brethren in other lands, have become expensive collectors' items.

Moving across the Alps into Austria, we find that the influence of the German flat, as might be expected, was strong throughout the 19th century. Around 1870, Joseph Sichart, a Viennese, began manufacturing 42 millimeter semiround figures of Austrian troops. The models included soldiers, bandsmen, and mounted officers of the famed Hoch und Deutschmeister Regiment. Foot figures were cast in one piece, but the mounted soldiers were detachable from the horses. The Sichart firm, founded in 1825 and now the oldest tin-casting firm in Vienna, still produces figures from the original molds. Toward the end of the 19th century, a Bavarian named Michael Wollner, having served an apprenticeship in the toy soldier factories of Nuremberg, relocated to Vienna. There, in the 1880s, he established his own firm and within a few years was producing a varied line of semi- and fully round figures celebrating the *belle époque* splendor of the Austro-Hungarian Empire in its final days of glory.

Like Heyde, Wollner made his figures in various sizes: semiround figures were 30, 38, or 45 millimeters. The Austro-Hungarian Army of Emperor Franz Josef received the greatest attention, and there were strikingly uniformed parade units from various parts of the empire, among them Jaegers and Landwehr in their distinctive Tyrolean caps and plumed royal guards and men-at-arms. Then, too, there were big brass bands with such charming touches as bass drums drawn by ponies or dogs, and a host of brilliantly garbed cavalrymen—dragoons, hussars, and lancers—the whole array presided over by equestrian figures of the emperor Franz Josef and his staff. Marching troops have an aggressive stride, reminiscent of Lucotte; and the cavalrymen are detachable from their mounts, with separately cast saddle trappings as well.

Greater diversity in pose is found in the smaller semiround figures. Here one sees troops vigorously attacking, and manning machine guns and artillery pieces, as well as work parties, field kitchens, and all manner of horse-drawn transport. Mindful of his origins, Wollner issued a range of Bavarian and Prussian troops of the period, among them such elite units as the Garde du Corps and Garde Uhlans; and there were even occasional sets of British, French, and American soldiers. Among the Wollner figures illustrated in Hans Roer's *Bleisoldaten* are United States infantry from the period of the Spanish-American War, still in their original squarish black box.

Some of Wollner's most delightful creations were his civilian scenes, evoking the spirit of Old Vienna. Elegantly dressed ladies and gentlemen promenade through parks, sip coffee at the ubiquitous cafés, or gather round a music pavillion to listen to a band concert. There were more than 100 different civilian types, including a range of railroad figures and others depicting fairy-tale characters such as Little Red Riding Hood and the Big Bad Wolf.

Wollner continued to operate his workshop until his death around the time of World War I. During the interwar years, production was continued by his daughter Adele, with some additional figures being added to the line. Around 1930, the molds were sold to another miniature soldier maker named Posnicker. When Nazi forces occupied Vienna in 1938, orders were given to destroy all vestiges of the old Austro-Hungarian Empire that might compete with the new German Reich. Toy soldiers were not exempt; and in order to prevent their confiscation and destruction, the Wollner molds were hidden ingeniously—they were used as paving blocks in the courtyard of an old house. They were reclaimed after the war and eventually were sold to Kober Spielwaren, Vienna's oldest and most distinguished toy store.

In the 1960s, Kober began reissuing Wollner figures cast from the original molds. Production continues today, although on a much smaller scale than in the prewar years. An American who visited the shop a few years ago

A squad of the famed Italian Bersaglieri by FIGIR, a Rome-based company that began manufacturing toy soldiers between the two world wars.
Henry Kurtz Collection   Height: 54 mm

This Italian engineer officer of the 1860s is a
good example of the generally high quality of
FIGIR's toy soldiers.
Henry Kurtz Collection   Height: 54 mm

A mounted officer by ISA, another Italian firm, whose figures were less refined than those of FIGIR.
Henry Kurtz Collection   Height: 75 mm

reported that it was "a collector's paradise in which we were transported back to the long ago days of pre–World War I Vienna. On the shelves were [figures of] Franz Josef and his ill-fated beautiful wife, Empress Elizabeth, ladies and gentlemen of the court, Household Guards, staff officers, cavalry in camp, and bands by the score—both on the march and playing on bandstands. Indeed, all the pomp, color, and majesty of the old Austro-Hungarian monarchy."

Like some other small European nations, Belgium imported most of its toy soldiers from Germany, France, and Great Britain. But in the 1930s, a local model maker named Emmanuel Steinback brought out a series of excellent figures, mainly of the French Army of the Napoleonic Wars. Steinback's firm was called MIM (Maximus in Minimus); in addition to Napoleonic troops, it issued British and United States soldiers of World War II and a small range of ancients—Egyptians, Assyrians, Persians, Romans, and Gauls. The figures were extremely sturdy and a bit larger than standard size—60 millimeters for foot and 80 millimeters for mounted figures. MIMs were really more model soldiers than toys, but because they bear some resemblance to the finer offerings of Lucotte, Mignot, and Haffner—in the best sense of quality casting and painting—it does not seem inappropriate to pay a small tribute to them here. The firm had a short life, production ending in 1948, and its figures are now much sought after and quite expensive when available.

Two small nations that did develop fairly significant local manufacturers of toy soldiers were Denmark and its Scandinavian neighbour Sweden. In Denmark, the home of Hans Christian Andersen's "Steadfast Toy Soldier," domestic production did not begin until the middle of the 19th century. Earlier flat figures of a harlequin, a shepherdess, and several other civilian and military types, one of which is dated 1796, are most likely of German origin. It is believed that a Danish pewterer may have obtained the molds—now in the Danish National Museum—from a German source and then used them to produce figures for local distribution.

The first known Danish manufacturer was a man named Hoy who began casting toy soldiers in the 1840s. His best-known model is an equestrian figure of King Frederick VII, which dates from around 1850. Based on the statue of King Frederick in Christiansborg Palace, it shows the monarch dressed in his cavalry uniform as colonel of the Danish Mounted Life Guard (Danske Livgarde til Hest) and wearing his special aluminum helmet. For the most part, however, toy soldiers were imported from Germany throughout the 19th and early 20th centuries until World War II, with Heyde figures predominating.

It was not until after World War II, when, as a Danish source cryptically notes, "it was no longer possible to trade with Germany," that native Danish producers blossomed. In the 1940s, two firms, Banner-Model and Brigader-Statuette, issued fully round solids that were 45 to 50 millimeters in scale. Of the two, Brigader was the more significant, its founder Carl Andersen mainly reworking Heyde models, but with original touches of his own and with far superior paintwork. An assortment of historical and contemporary soldiers was offered, including Danish, German, and British troops of World War II in action poses. Historical types concentrated on Danish units of the late 19th century, a particularly charming vignette consisting of a group of Danish staff officers surrounding a map table, with the cap belonging to a bareheaded officer perched atop the table.

Andersen lavished his greatest attention on the Danish Life Guard, the royal foot guard regiment founded in 1658. The regiment was depicted both in its everyday blue full-dress uniform and the scarlet ceremonial dress worn only on special occasions. Undoubtedly the most original of Andersen's models, though still showing the Heyde influence, the guardsmen were issued in a variety of postures—marching, standing at attention, and in the at-ease position of the sentries at Amalienborg Palace. A full band with complete instrumentation was available and could be had in scarlet or blue dress, at attention or marching. An excellent selection of the different versions of Brigader's

Beginning in the 1880s, Michael Wollner, trained in Nuremberg,
began issuing soldiers of the Austro-Hungarian Empire in various
sizes. Here we see mounted troops of the Austrian Landwehr.
Henry Kurtz Collection   Height: 65 mm

guards can be seen at the Danish Life Guard Museum in Copenhagen. Production of Brigader figures came to an end with the death of Carl Andersen a few years ago.

Aluminum figures were manufactured before World War II by a company called Rode-Orm. In 1946, another Danish firm, G. Krohn-Rasmussen, absorbed Rode-Orm and continued to issue its figures, along with models of their own, under the trademark Krolyn (although some figures still carried the old "Rode-Orm" mark). Consisting mainly of Viking warriors, medieval knights, and some models obviously inspired by the film versions of Robin Hood and Ivanhoe, these well-designed and nicely paint-ed figures were roughly the same size as American dime-store soldiers—75 to 80 millimeters. Particularly fine is the series of wonderfully animated Viking types, the figures vividly portraying the ferocity and physical strength of the old Norse warriors.

Although some flats were made in Sweden in the late 1700s, there was no serious commercial manufacture of toy soldiers until the latter years of the 19th century, when Santessonska Tenngjuteriet (founded in 1839) began issu-ing flats and, later, semiround and three-dimensional toy troops in various sizes. Molds for their early flat figures are believed to have originated in Germany, as did many of those for their semisolid models. Santessonska's toy soldiers were widely distributed throughout Sweden and the firm had its own shop in Stockholm. Its semisolid range featured a popular historical series highlighting important battles in Swedish military history—among them Narva and Lützen. A peculiarity of the semiround figures was the production of horses in two pieces—front and back being cast separately. Semi- and fully round mounted figures came with detachable riders; and, in the case of their three-dimensional series of royal personalities, the saddle trappings were also detachable. In 1924, the company's name was changed to Gamla Tenngjuteriet Holmberg & Bjorck. The firm survived until 1964, but lead soldier pro-duction ceased in the 1930s.

C. C. Ohlssons Leksaksfabrik, another Stockholm-based firm, produced tin soldiers and other tin toys on a modest scale, with painting being done by homeworkers. Flat, semiround, and fully round figures, mostly of simple design, were cast from molds acquired in Germany. Besides Swedish troops, they are known to have issued soldiers of the armies involved in World War I. After relocating to Tidaholm in 1937, the firm slowly phased out its toy soldier production in the 1940s.

The third of Sweden's principal firms, described by a Swedish source as an "ambitious, well-operated company with a first-class production line," was Tenngjuteriet Mars, which began manufacturing toy soldiers in 1915. Their spirited 30- and 40-millimeter flats not only enjoyed the greatest popularity in Sweden, where the firm's output soon outstripped that of its rivals, but they were also exported to Denmark and Russia. Since Mars began operations in the midst of World War I, its first offerings were troops of the participating nations in that conflict, plus those of Sweden and Denmark. But the firm's most interesting models were the beautifully designed histori-cal and ethnographic ranges. Prominent among the latter were village scenes of Swedish Lapps, North American Indians, and Central African native peoples. These were the work of Ossian Elgstrom, who was also responsible for a delightful series depicting Swedish farm life, inspired by the books of a local author named Anna Maria Roos. Mars remained in business until the 1960s, but toy soldier pro-duction was terminated before World War II. (It is worth noting that many of the molds from the three Swedish firms are now in the possession of Ake Dahlback, founder and curator of the Tennfigur Museum in Leksand, Sweden. Figures cast from these molds and painted by Dahlback are occasionally sold at the museum's gift shop.)

Across the Baltic Sea in Russia, wooden and paper soldiers were popular in the 18th and 19th centuries and were produced locally; but metal figures, including those in the large collection of Czar Peter III, were imported from Germany. In the early 1900s, some domestic manufacture of 40-millimeter flats took place, the local firms focusing on such contemporary Russian military

Denmark's leading toy soldier maker was Brigader-Statuette, which
started up after World War II. Heyde-like in appearance, the firm's
toy troops included bandsmen of the Danish Life Guard (shown here
in their scarlet ceremonial uniforms).
Henry Kurtz Collection   Height: 48 mm

A fierce Viking warrior by Krolyn, a Danish firm that made aluminum toy soldiers.
Henry Kurtz Collection   Height: 75 mm

Swedish Royal Guardsmen in turn-of-the-century uniforms, reproduced from original Santessonska molds by Sweden's Tennfigur Museum.
Henry Kurtz Collection   Height: 45 mm

The most prolific of the Swedish toy soldier makers was
Tenngjuteriet Mars, whose line of 30mm and 40mm flats included
these British troops and Dutch Boers from the South African war.
Henry Kurtz Collection

involvements as the Russo–Turkish and Russo–Japanese wars. According to one commentator, the figures were "cast in soft metal [and] gaudily painted. The cavalrymen had lances of wire which were inserted into the mold prior to the casting of the figure, and which bent at the slightest touch." Many models appear to have been crude copies of German toy soldiers, one firm going so far as to issue its piracies in Heinrichsen-style boxes. Between the world wars, some poor-quality solids were turned out, and at a 1950s trade fair in East Germany, Russian-made tin and wooden figures were on exhibit. More recently, visitors to GUM, Moscow's leading department store, reported seeing some flat and semiround metal figures of Russian troops. Figures in hard plastic are now made and these show contemporary Soviet soldiers heroically postured in the best tradition of Socialist Realism. All things considered, and given Russia's long imperial past, its production of toy soldiers has not been distinguished.

Among non-Western nations, Japan is the only one known to have had any substantial involvement in the manufacture of metal soldiers. The earliest mention of Japanese-made toy soldiers so far uncovered, cited by J. G. Garratt in his *World Encyclopedia of Model Soldiers*, appears in the 1914 catalogue of Butler Brothers, an American toy dealer. Under the heading "Miscellaneous Japanese Toys," mention is made of a set of 10 papier-mâché soldiers and sailors, $2\frac{1}{4}$ inches in height, representing Japanese military and naval units. If other firms existed, their products do not seem to have made any impact outside of Japan.

During the Allied occupation of Japan after World War II, a few Japanese firms such as Sonsco produced boxed sets of hollow-cast toy soldiers, including some with movable arms, that were usually copies of British-made models. But one firm eventually went beyond mere piracy to issue an interesting range of metal figures under the trade name Minikin or Minikins (both designations appearing on boxes). Just where in Japan the figures originated remains a mystery, but the exclusive American distributor was International Models, a New York–based importer. Research by Will Beierwaltes indicates that this company had been in existence since the 1920s and that it specialized in hobby goods. Except for some Britains models, Minikins appear to be the only toy soldiers handled by the firm.

Reference to Minikins first appears in International Models' 1949 catalogue, and that, at present, is as close as we can come to dating the beginnings of this line. Ambitiously, Minikins set out to cover a wide span of history, from the days when Hannibal and his war elephants crossed the Alps to 19th- and 20th-century military types. Some of the first offerings included 15th-century knights that were copies of Britains models, while an individual Norman knight was blatantly lifted from Richard Courtenay's "Battle of Poitiers" series of fighting knights. Even their most attractive boxed set, "Hannibal's War Elephant," consisted mainly of reworked Heyde models of ancient Romans.

However, side by side with the pirated models were originals of considerable merit, well designed and well painted. Among these we find a series of figures depicting Scottish regiments based on wooden figures sculpted by Pilkington Jackson for the military museum at Edinburgh Castle; and another grouping of French troops of World War I and of the period immediately preceding World War II.

Unquestionably the finest Minikins were those of samurai warriors of the 12th and 13th centuries. Dramatic in pose—particularly a mounted samurai on a plunging horse—the three early models were exquisitely rendered, the foot figures having detachable weapons. Later figures of 17th-century samurai were more static in posture but exhibited the same excellent brushwork found in the previous models. Equally notable are several portrait figures of historical personalities, among them an equestrian model of Napoleon, based on Jacques-Louis David's well-known painting of Bonaparte crossing the Alps, and another of the Mongol chieftain Tamerlane. Two historical models of British regiments are interesting in that they were scrupulously copied from period illustra-

Dragoon, 1815

During the late 1940s the Japanese firm of Minikin began producing
both toy and model soldiers like this British dragoon of the
Napoleonic Wars, which was based on an old military print.
Henry Kurtz Collection   Height: 75 mm

tions reproduced in James Laver's *British Military Uniforms*, first published in 1948. One shows a private of the Coldstream Guards, 1742, the other a British dragoon of 1815.

Naturally, the American market received a full measure of attention. Included here were a series of military units of the American Revolutionary War, and a lively representation of the "Spirit of '76," which was issued in a box bearing a label with the opening musical notes and words of "Yankee Doodle Dandy." At the time of the sesquicentennial (in 1952) of the founding of the U. S. Military Academy at West Point, Minikins brought out a figure in the original 1802 uniform of the Regiment of Artillerists and Engineers and another in 1952 full dress. These and a rather awkward U. S. Horse Marine of 1900 mounted on a ridiculously undersized horse are among the least noteworthy of the firm's models.

In size, Minikins ranged from about 45 millimeters (in the case of the pirated Heydes) to roughly 60 millimeters for the special-unit models (most figures being in the 54 to 60 mm scale). Various designations appear under the bases. During the period of Allied occupation, Japanese goods exported to the United States had to clearly state that they were made in Japan. Thus early Minikins are marked "Occupied Japan" or "Made in Occupied Japan," while figures issued after 1952 have the words "Made in Japan" or, more often, "IMP-Japan" engraved on the underside of the dark-green bases. The IMP may have been an abbreviation for "imported" or perhaps "International Model Products." The better-quality models came in small gray boxes stamped "Minikins" or sometimes bearing, on a small gold label, the designation "Tru-Detail. Mini-Kins. International Models. N. Y. City."

Minikin figures enjoyed a fair degree of popularity in their day but were not as extensively produced or as widely distributed as those of their European competitors. It may well be, as Will Beierwaltes suggests, that Minikin tried to do too much by producing some models as children's toys and others as "military miniatures" for adult collectors of model soldiers, then a new and growing market. "In fact, having straddled this fence," observes Beierwaltes, "they may have failed to satisfy either marketplace, and therefore slipped into their relative obscurity."

That the firm continued to produce throughout the 1950s is borne out by listings in catalogues from Polk's in New York, Corr's in Washington, D.C., and other specialized dealerships. Minikins were still being sold in some hobby stores in the early 1960s, but whether these figures were current production or remaining stock is unclear. What is fairly certain is that escalating labor and material costs, child safety laws, and competition from cheaper plastic toys had the same effect on Minikin as they had on lead soldier manufacturers in other countries. Yet although its life span was short and the number of different models it produced barely exceeded 50, Minikin is worthy of recognition among that select group of makers from different lands who sent forth battalions of miniature troops during the two centuries in which the metal toy soldier reigned supreme.

Jacques Louis David's painting of Napoleon crossing the Alps
inspired this Minikin figure of the French military leader.
Henry Kurtz Collection   Height: 75 mm

For the American market, Minikin produced a three-dimensional
representation of the "Spirit of '76."
Henry Kurtz Collection   Height: 60 mm

Conclusion

The metal toy soldier is now a plaything of the past. Driven from the playroom by toy safety laws, routed from department store shelves by an overwhelming horde of cheaper plastic figures, the traditional lead and tin toy troops that captivated generations of youngsters have become museum pieces or highly prized—and highly priced— collectibles. But not everyone bemoans the demise of the old toy soldier, for there have always been those who derided him for allegedly fostering militaristic impulses in pliable youngsters.

Even a century ago, when the metal toy soldier was at the height of its popularity, critics were plentiful. In the 1860s, George A. Sala, a prominent English journalist, lashed out against the flood of "bellicose playthings" pouring out of the German states. While praising the peaceful toys produced by other European nations, Sala denounced "the fierce martial display of Bavaria, Hesse, and Wurtemberg. . . . Those misguided small Germans! Much better would it have been had they thrown themselves into tiny locomotives and hansom cabs and windmills."

Lest it be thought that Sala and his ilk were merely venting anti-German prejudices, verbal broadsides were also unleashed against Britain's traditional enemy across the Channel. In an article dated December 16, 1872, the *London Graphic* accused the French of using military toys "as a sort of elementary training to fire the war spirit of the nation." Not to be outdone, the French turned right around and fired a few salvos of their own—at the nasty Germans across the Rhine. The firm of Heinrichsen was singled out by one French journal for "instilling into the minds of the young the bravery, the might, and the glory of the German army."

In truth, there is nothing to suggest that toy soldiers have had any substantial influence on the later career choices of those who played with them (notwithstanding Winston Churchill's remarks, quoted earlier); nor is there any evidence that toy soldiers have been a principal factor in releasing otherwise dormant martial instincts. As one writer keenly observed, "every girl who nurses her doll does not become a Florence Nightingale, nor is there in later life an overwhelming desire to be engine drivers on the part of the boys . . . who play with miniature trains." Quite the contrary, barely a handful of today's toy soldier enthusiasts—who number in the thousands and include virtually every major civil occupation and profession—are active or former professional military men.

Far from being an encouragement to jingoism, playing with toy soldiers has been seen by some as cathartic—a release of hostile aggression that might otherwise be directed at one's fellow beings. That, at any rate, was the viewpoint of H. G. Wells, who saw "little war" as a moral substitute for real war. Wells elaborated on this theme in the conclusion of his now-classic *Little Wars*. "How much better is this amiable miniature than the Real Thing!" he maintained. "Here is the premeditation, the thrill, the strain of accumulating victory or disaster—and no smashed nor sanguinary bodies, no shattered fine buildings nor devastated countryside, no petty cruelties . . . that we who are old enough to remember a real modern war know to be the reality of belligerence. This world is for ample living . . . all of us in every country, except a few dull-witted, energetic bores, want to see the manhood of the world at something better than aping the little lead toys our children buy in boxes."

Continuing, Wells offered his modest solution to the

problem of real war: ". . . let us put this prancing monarch and that silly scaremonger, and those excitable 'patriots' and those adventurers, and all the practitioners of *Welt Politik*, into one vast Temple of War, with cork carpets everywhere, and plenty of little trees and little houses to knock down, and cities and fortresses, and unlimited [toy] soldiers—tons, cellars-full,—and let them lead their own lives there away from us."

What a splendid idea. Unfortunately, it is as impractical as it is wonderful. Alas, the power-hungry practitioners of real war are unlikely to be satisfied with miniature metal substitutes for the flesh-and-blood warriors they push around the world's battlefields. And anyway, the old toy soldier is no more—he has faded away. Well, not completely. In recent years, to meet a growing demand by toy soldier enthusiasts, manufacturers in Great Britain and the United States have begun to produce metal toy soldiers in the traditional manner—handpainted in glossy enamels and even with movable arms. However, because of the prohibition against the use of lead in toys, they are intended for collectors rather than children. They are also expensive, with sets of from four to eight figures costing $30 to $60, sometimes much more.

Nostalgia plays an important role in what are sometimes called "new old toy soldiers," and indeed when Shamus Wade began a trend in 1974, he called his line "Nostalgia Models." Wade's focus was British Empire forces of the Victorian era. In fact, colorfully uniformed units of the late-19th-century British Army and allied colonial troops dominate the lists of most of the small firms that have sprung up in Nostalgia's wake. Today there are more than thirty new toy soldier makers, with others turning up each year. The majority are located in Great Britain, where such martial-sounding names as Marlborough, British Bulldog, Steadfast Soldiers, All the Queen's Men, and Militia Models evoke memories of past imperial glory. In the United States, Limited Edition Miniatures, Edmund's Traditional Toy Soldiers, and Marcat Miniatures issue figures of United States troops, while others like Quartermaster Corps and Brigade Miniatures concentrate on British Army and colonial forces. Worth mentioning also are Imperial Productions of New Zealand, Trophy of Wales, and Brigadier Miniatures in Australia. All of these companies produce figures of outstanding quality, in many ways superior—and certainly more imaginative—than those of the old toy soldier makers in whose footsteps they follow.

Nearly all of the new breed of manufacturers are family-owned and family-operated small businesses—often a sideline to other occupations. Interestingly, the making of metal toy soldiers, which began as a cottage industry in the 18th century and evolved into a mass-production business in the aftermath of the Industrial Revolution, has come full cycle and is now, once more, a cottage industry. So the parade of the metal toy soldiers marches on. Only now they are no longer playthings to amuse children; they are made primarily for the pleasure of adults, or perhaps, put another way, the child that lurks within us all.

Bibliography

Books on Toy and Model Soldiers

Baldet, Marcel. *Figurines et Soldats de Plomb*. New York: Crown Publishers, 1961.

Bard, Bob. *Making and Collecting Military Miniatures*. New York: Robert M. McBride Company, 1957.

Boesgaard, Nils Eric. *Tingelinge-later tinsoldater*. Copenhagen: Thejls Bogtryk, 1966.

Cadbury, Betty. *Playthings Past: A Collector's Guide to Antique Toys*. New York: Praeger Publishers, 1976.

Carman, W. Y. *Model Soldiers*. London: Charles Letts and Company, 1972.

Garratt, John G. *Model Soldiers: A Collector's Guide*. London: Seeley, Service & Company, Ltd., 1959, 1965.

———. *Model Soldiers: An Illustrated History*. Greenwich, Conn.: New York Graphic Society, 1972.

———. *Collecting Model Soldiers*. New York: Arco Publishing Company, 1975.

———. *The World Encyclopedia of Model Soldiers*. London: Frederick Muller Ltd., 1981.

Hampe, Theodor. *Der Zinnsoldat*. Reprint of the original 1924 edition. Berlin: Bernd Ehrig, 1982.

Harris, Major Henry. *Model Soldiers*. London: Octopus Books Ltd., 1972.

Johnson, Peter. *Toy Armies*. London: B. T. Batsford Ltd., 1981.

Keester, George, and Rolf Nelson. *Soldats de Plomb: Part I, 1890–1920*. Privately printed, 1980.

McKenzie, Ian. *Collecting Old Toy Soldiers*. London: B. T. Batsford Ltd., 1975.

O'Brien, Richard. *Collecting Toys*. Florence, Ala.: Books Americana, 1982.

Opie, James. *Toy Soldiers*. Aylesbury, Eng.: Shire Publications Ltd., 1983.

Ortmann, Erwin. *The Collector's Guide to Model Tin Figures*. New York: G. P. Putnam's Sons, 1974.

Pielen, Don. *The American Dimestore Soldier Book: An Illustrated Guide*. Privately printed, 1983.

Polaine, Reggie. *The War Toys: The Story of Hausser-Elastolin*. London: New Cavendish Books, 1979.

Richards, L. W. *Old British Model Soldiers, 1893–1918*. London: Arms and Armour Press, 1970.

Roer, Hans H. *Bleisoldaten*. Munich: George D. W. Callwey, 1981.

Ruddell, Joanne and Ron. *The Britains Collector's Checklist*. 3 vols. Allentown, Pa.: Privately printed, 1980–82.

Ruddle, John. *Collectors' Guide to Britains Model Soldiers*. Watford, Eng.: Model and Allied Publications, Argus Books Ltd., 1980.

Taylor, Arthur. *Discovering Model Soldiers*. Aylesbury, Eng.: Shire Publications Ltd., 1972.

Wallis, Joe. *Regiments of All Nations*. Baltimore: Privately printed, 1981.

Wells, H. G. *Little Wars*. London: J. M. Dent and Sons Ltd., 1931.

Books on Military History and Uniforms

Barnes, Major R. Money. *A History of the Regiments & Uniforms of the British Army*. London: Seeley, Service & Company, Ltd., 1950.

Carman, W. Y. *A Dictionary of Military Uniform*. New York: Charles Scribner's Sons, 1977.

Cassin-Scott, Jack, and John Fabb. *Ceremonial Uniforms of the World*. New York: Arco Publishing Company, 1977.

Coggins, Jack. *The Fighting Man*. New York: Doubleday & Company, 1966.

Farwell, Byron. *Mr. Kipling's Army*. New York: W. W. Norton & Company, 1981.

Kannik, Preben. *Military Uniforms of the World in Color*. New York: Macmillan, Inc., 1968.

Laver, James. *British Military Uniforms*. London: Penguin Books Ltd., 1948.

North, Rene. *Military Uniforms, 1698–1918*. New York: Bantam Books, 1971.

Ropp, Theodore. *War in the Modern World*. New York: Collier Books, 1962.

Walton, Lt. Col. P. S. *Simkin's Soldiers: Vol I—The British Army in 1890*. Dorking, Eng.: Victorian Military Society, 1981.

Wilkinson-Latham, R. J. *Collecting Militaria*. New York: Arco Publishing Company, 1975.

Wilson, Lt. Col. Frank. *Regiments at a Glance*. London: Blackie & Sons, Ltd., 1955.

Magazine Articles, Periodicals, and Other Publications

Asquith, Stuart. "Collecting New Toy Soldiers." *Military Modelling* (August 1982).

"Invasion of the Toy Battalions." *Antiques & Art* (Canada) (December 1979, January 1980).

Kurtz, Henry I. "In Search of Those Profitable Playthings." *Antiques & Collectibles* (June 1980).

———. "Little Toy Soldiers." *The New Book of Knowledge Annual*, 1980.

———. "Old Toy Soldiers: The Rise of the Britains Empire." *Campaigns*, no. 34 (May–June 1981).

———. "Toy Soldier Exhibit at West Point Museum." *The Bulletin*, no. 3 (1982).

———. "Toy Soldiers Never Die, They Just Turn to Profit." *American Way* (December 1979).

McAfee, Michael J. *The Toy Soldier: An Historical Review*. Catalogue of an exhibit of toy soldiers at the West Point Museum. *West Point Museum Bulletin*, 5 (March 1982).

Morner, Aimée L. "A Joyful Clash of Arms." *Fortune* (Dec. 18, 1979).

Old Toy Soldier Newsletter. Vols. I–IX.

The Richards Collection of Lead Soldiers and Figures. Phillips Sale 23,469 catalogue, held in London, August 12 and 13, 1981.

Scrine, T. J. *A Short History of Britains Ltd*. In-house publication, 1955.

Shumach, Murray. "It's a Small World." *Antiques World* (April 1979).

Tennfigur Museum catalogue. Includes notes on Swedish toy soldier companies by Ake Dahlback. Leksand, Sweden, 1979.

Also selected articles from *The Bulletin*, the journal of the British Model Soldier Society; *Guidon*, the journal of the Miniature Figure Collectors of America; and *The Vedette*, journal of the National Capital Military Collectors.

Manufacturer's Catalogues

Britains Ltd. catalogues for 1885, 1908, 1923, 1936, 1939, 1953, 1958, 1966, and 1983.

Charbens & Company Ltd. catalogue for 1960.

Cherilea Products catalogue for 1956.

Crescent Toy Company Ltd. catalogue for 1940.

Georg Heyde Company catalogue for 1925.

Johillco catalogue for 1939.

Timpo catalogue for 1950.

In addition to the above sources, correspondence with Holger Eriksson, Peter Johnson, George Keester, Michael McAfee, Richard O'Brien, and Roy Selwyn-Smith. Collection of the author.

Illustration Date Indicator

Compiled by James Opie

The dates given below indicate when the toy soldiers illustrated were first manufactured. Some toy soldiers were produced in the same style for many years, so in several cases the date is not exactly the one for the soldier illustrated. Page numbers are given in boldface. All locations noted (left, right, etc.) refer to the position of the picture on the page. Whenever soldiers of differing dates appear in the same picture, their dates are identified moving from left to right within the picture.

Frontispiece, 1905; **10,** 1925; **14,** 1900; **16** (top), 1880; **16** (middle), 1880; **16** (bottom), 1890; **17,** 1900; **19,** 1870; **20** (left), 1890; **20** (right), 1890; **21,** 1905; **23** (top), 1900; **23** (bottom), 1910; **24,** 1910; **25,** 1900; **27** (left), 1900, 1949; **27** (right), 1925; **28,** 1910; **29,** 1925; **31** (top), 1925; **31** (bottom), 1925; **32,** 1910; **33,** 1910; **35,** 1910; **36,** 1920; **37** (top), 1900; **37** (bottom), 1920; **39,** 1920; **40,** 1910; **41** (top), 1905; **41** (bottom), 1920; **43,** 1905, 1925; **44,** 1925; **45,** 1900; **46,** 1935; **47** (top), 1902; **47** (bottom), 1910; **48,** 1930; **49,** 1905; **50,** 1900; **51,** 1920; **52,** 1900; **54,** 1905; **55,** 1890; **57** (top), 1903; **57** (bottom), 1900; **58,** 1900; **59** (top), 1905; **59** (bottom), 1930; **61** (top), 1950; **61** (bottom), 1955; **62,** 1950; **63** (top); 1960; **63** (bottom), 1955; **65,** 1930; **66,** 1930; **67** (top), 1925; **67** (bottom), 1955; **69** (top); 1955; **69** (bottom), 1950; **70,** 1930; **71,** 1930; **73** (top), 1905; **73** (bottom), 1930; **74,** 1918; **75** (top), 1925; **75** (bottom), 1920; **77,** 1920; **78** (top), 1930; **78** (bottom), 1925; **79** (top), 1910; **79** (bottom), 1910; **81** (top), 1910; **81** (bottom), 1910; **82** (top), 1930; **82** (middle), 1930; **82** (bottom), 1930; **83,** 1930; **85** (top

left), 1950; **85** (top right), 1950; **85** (bottom), 1955; **86** (top left), 1955; **86** (top right), 1955; **86** (bottom), 1955; **87,** 1955; **89** (left), 1955; **89** (right), 1955; **90,** 1960; **91** (top), 1960; **91** (bottom), 1935; **93** (top), 1900; **93** (bottom), 1955; **94** (top left), 1955; **94** (top right), 1955; **94** (bottom left), 1955; **94** (bottom right), 1955; **95** (top), 1930; **95** (bottom), 1930; **96,** 1930; **97,** 1935; **98,** 1912; **99** (top), 1948; **99** (bottom left), 1950; **99** (bottom right), 1948; **100,** 1897; **102,** 1890; **103,** 1890; **105,** 1910; **106,** 1895; **107,** 1890; **110,** 1910; **111** (top), 1895; **111** (bottom), 1948, 1932; **113,** 1909; **115** (top), 1900; **115** (bottom), 1925; **116,** 1899; **117,** 1930; **118,** 1900; **119,** 1906; **120,** 1933; **121,** 1896; **122,** 1920; **123,** 1930; **124,** 1935, 1905; **125** (left), 1896; **125** (right), 1935; **127,** 1920; **128** (top), 1900; **128** (bottom), 1955; **130,** 1896; **131,** 1908; **132,** 1900; **133,** 1900; **134,** 1933, 1899; **135,** 1910; **136,** 1900; **137,** 1922; **138,** 1938; **139,** 1940; **140,** 1912; **141** (top), 1956, 1930, 1905; **141** (bottom), 1930; **142** (top), 1930, 1905; **142** (bottom), 1901, 1914; **143** (top), 1900; **143** (bottom), 1926; **144,** 1897; **145,** 1900, 1928; **146,** 1902; **147,** 1907; **148,** 1916; **149,** 1905, 1910; **150** (top), 1940,

1908, 1920; **150** (bottom), 1940; **151** (top), 1920; **151** (bottom), 1914, 1930; **152,** 1920; **153,** 1940; **154,** 1938, 1928, 1908; **155,** 1935; **156** (top), 1938; **156** (bottom), 1930; **157,** 1915; **158,** 1928; **159,** 1937, 1925; **162,** 1910; **163** (top), 1940; **163** (bottom), 1940; **164,** 1938; **165,** 1939; **167,** 1940; **168,** 1939; **170,** 1938; **171,** 1939; **172** (top), 1939; **172** (bottom), 1912; **173** (top), 1939; **173** (bottom), 1937; **174,** 1954; **175,** 1954; **176** (top), 1939; **176** (bottom), 1935; **177,** 1939; **178,** 1955; **179,** 1935; **181,** 1897, 1901; **182** (top), 1908; **182** (bottom), 1929; **183** (top), 1940; **183** (bottom), 1938; **184,** 1938; **185,** 1937; **186** (top), 1927; **186** (bottom), 1955; **187,** 1928; **189** (top), 1905, 1955; **189** (bottom), 1922, 1932; **190** (top), 1940; **190** (bottom), 1940; **191** (bottom), 1939; **192,** 1940; **193,** 1938; **194,** 1946; **195** (top), 1932; **195** (bottom), 1935; **196** (top), 1927; **196** (bottom), 1935; **197** (top), 1940; **197** (bottom), 1899, 1906; **198** (top), 1932; **198** (bottom), 1930; **199** (top), 1932; **199** (bottom), 1937; **201,** 1947; **202** (top), 1955; **202** (bottom), 1940; **203** (top), 1940; **203** (bottom), 1939; **204,** 1940; **206** (top), 1940; **206** (bottom), 1937-1958; **207,** 1938; **208,** 1939; **209,** 1938; **210,** 1958; **213,**

1954; **214** (top), 1959; **214** (bottom), 1953; **215** (top), 1955; **215,** (bottom), 1957; **216** (top), 1957; **216** (bottom), 1956; **218,** 1956; **220,** 1965; **223,** 1953; **224,** 1953; **225** (left), 1940; **225** (right), 1953; **227,** 1953; **229,** 1952; **230,** 1952; **233,** 1952; **234,** 1952; **235,** 1952; **236,** 1938; **238,** 1865; **239** (left) 1917; **239** (right), 1917; **241,** 1905; **242** (top), 1923; **242** (bottom), 1925; **243,** 1937; **245,** 1937-1955; **246,** 1937; **247,** 1937; **249,** 1939; **250,** 1950; **251,** 1939; **253,** 1939; **254,** 1939; **255,** 1950; **257** (left), 1936; **257** (right), 1936; **258** (left), 1937; **258** (right), 1937; **259,** 1939; **261,** 1939; **262,** 1939; **263,** 1939; **265,** 1939; **266,** 1939; **267,** 1939; **269,** 1945; **270,** 1939; **271,** 1939; **273,** 1946; **274,** 1917; **275,** 1936; **277,** 1949; **278** (left), 1937; **278** (right), 1927; **279,** 1938; **281,** 1939; **282,** 1938; **283,** 1938; **285,** 1938; **286,** 1938; **287,** 1938; **289,** 1948; **290,** 1948; **291,** 1948; **293;** 1948; **294,** 1948; **295,** 1948; **296,** 1948; **297,** 1948; **298,** 1948; **299,** 1948; **300,** 1948; **301,** 1955; **302,** 1900; **305,** 1936; **306,** 1936; **307,** 1930; **309,** 1900; **311,** 1950; **312** (top), 1950; **312** (bottom), 1980; **313,** 1915; **315,** 1950; **317,** 1950; **318,** 1950

Index